# Praise

"Blunt, eloquent, piercing, honest, witty, heartaching, startlingly funny, and beautifully, refreshingly unique. Can you read a book about pain while grinning and trying not to cry and not being able to think of a single book that's anything like it? Yup. This one. *Guts*."
BRIAN DOYLE, AUTHOR OF *MINK RIVER*

"A beautiful and honest portrait of resilience and emotion along the winding path of a friendship woven with long-term health issues. Janet Buttenwieser writes with a keen eye not only about medical challenges but also places these challenges in their rightful place among the supports of friendship, love, career, and community. Buttenwieser's clear prose shares confidences like a friend, and I found this book difficult to put down."
SONYA HUBER, AUTHOR OF *PAIN WOMAN TAKES YOUR KEYS AND OTHER ESSAYS FROM A NERVOUS SYSTEM*

"GUTS is a fearless memoir about the limits of the body and the strength of the spirit. Janet Buttenwieser's journey through chronic illness, infertility, and loss will resonate with anyone who's ever wondered why bad news always comes in waves. Her grit and sense of humour make this an unforgettable story."
LEIGH STEIN, AUTHOR OF *LAND OF ENCHANTMENT*

"You'll be hooked from the very first scene, intrigued by the story's promise: a woman's decisive, tenacious journey through illness and loss. This book is about friendship, family, and the challenge to accept—and survive—the events in our lives beyond our control."
NICOLE HARDY, AUTHOR OF *CONFESSIONS OF A LATTER-DAY VIRGIN*

# About the Author

Janet Buttenwieser's work has appeared in *The Rumpus, Under the Sun, Potomac Review, The Pinch, Bellevue Literary Review*, and elsewhere. GUTS was a finalist for the University of New Orleans Publishing Lab Prize. Her work has been nominated for a Pushcart Prize, was a finalist for Oregon Quarterly's Northwest Perspectives Essay Contest, and won honourable mention in The Atlantic Student Writing contest, the New Millennium Writings Award and the Artsmith Literary Award. She holds an MFA from the Northwest Institute of Literary Arts.

Visit Janet online: *janetbuttenwieser.com*

Print Edition
ISBN: 978-1-925417-64-7

Published by Vine Leaves Press 2018
Melbourne, Victoria, Australia

Cover images from konradbak and tets
Cover design by Jessica Bell
Interior design by Amie McCracken

National Library of Australia Cataloguing-in-Publication entry
(paperback)
Creator: Buttenwieser, Janet, author.
Title: Guts : a memoir / Janet Buttenwieser.
ISBN: 9781925417647 (paperback)
Subjects: Buttenwieser, Janet, Guts.
 Digestive organs--Patients--United States--Biography.
 Caregivers--United States--Biography.
 Cancer--Psychological aspects.
 Interpersonal relations--Bibliography.

For Nasus —
Here's to NILA, and to gutsy
women everywhere.

# GUTS

## Janet Buttenwieser

Warmly,

Janet B

**Vine Leaves Press**
Melbourne, Vic, Australia

# Table of Contents

Disclaimer:

I have tried to recreate events, locales and conversations from my memories of them. In order to maintain their anonymity in some instances I have changed the names of individuals and their identifying characteristics.

For Beth
Forever my hero, always my friend

# Prologue

September 12th, 2009

It was the middle of the triathlon as race volunteers prepared to eject me from the course. Eleven weeks, three days and seven hours since the moment time divided into before and after. As I pedalled uphill, I didn't consider the way my lycra outfit accentuated my colostomy pouch rather than concealing it, the hems of my shirt and shorts meeting at the place where surgical scars formed a lopsided tic-tac-toe board near my navel. I didn't think about my friend Beth. My mind wasn't even on my husband and children back home in Seattle. My brain focused on the clock: the hours that had gone by since the starting gun went off, the minutes remaining before the course would close, the seconds that would pass between the belief that I could make it, and the moment that I knew it was too late.

At dawn the world had been shrouded in fog. By mid-morning it had begun its slow retreat, the curtain inching upwards to reveal the craggy-rock Northern California coastline. In Seattle, we noticed the shortening of daylight, and foggy September mornings were common there, too. But this felt different, this cycling inside a cloud, the rain tiny needles pecking at my cheeks. The atmosphere pressed on me from all sides, like I was pedalling through honey someone had poured over my head and onto the road in front of me. In other words, I felt as I had for the previous six months as I cared for a newborn and a toddler, watched

Beth die—first slowly, then suddenly—and tried to navigate the days since. They were endless, those days, or they evaporated. What did I have to show for them? I'd kept my children alive. I'd made it to the starting line of a triathlon.

I'd trained for the race with a group. But triathlons aren't a team sport; on race day in California I was on my own, moving alongside people, but not with them. It was just me and the clock. No one told me that the clock always wins.

I crested the hill and looped around the turn, shifting and pedalling faster. This was my third lap of four and the repetition felt like being lost in a foreign city, trying to find a different road, but continuing to pass the same landmarks: the cluster of cheering teenagers ringing cowbells and blowing party horns, the Beachcomber Inn whose billboard announced "Best Summer Rates" through the veil of fog.

In a triathlon, racers get divided into groups according to age and gender. Typically, the professional athletes go first followed by the age groups—men, then women, young to old. The California race varied this order with the pros starting their race last instead of first, entering the water two hours after the last women's age group. Each section of the triathlon—the swim, then the bike, then the run—closed at a certain time so that the elite athletes could compete on a relatively empty course. The bike course was scheduled to close at 12:00. My heart dropped when I learnt this information the day before the race.

"I won't be finished biking by noon," I'd told the volunteer at the registration table.

"As long as you're on the course by then, you'll be fine," she said.

***

I took a bite of protein bar stored in a case on the top tube of my bike and chased it down with a few sips of energy drink from my water pack. The night before the race, I pinned a laminated photograph to the pack. In it, Beth sat in her kayak on the Washington coast. As I held the pack's straw in my mouth, a woman pedalled up behind me.

"Keep thinking about that person on your back that you're racing for," she said as she pulled alongside me, then ahead. "You're almost there."

I watched her pull away into the fog. She was right; I was racing in Beth's honour. Had she been there, Beth would have been the person to say something encouraging to an energy-flagging stranger. She would have helped me out at the registration table the day before, getting me placed in an earlier start group so I'd have more time. On that day, as with so many in the past, shyness tied my tongue. Apparently I still operated as though Beth were by my side, bolstering my confidence to assert myself. When would it sink in that she was really and truly gone?

I looked down at the Ironman-brand watch my husband Matt had given me one Christmas, the kids not yet born, triathlons a new hobby. 11:50. Two minutes later I approached the turnaround for my last lap, past a throng of people yelling loudly at their family members and friends. It wasn't until I was nearly to the turn that I noticed race volunteers waving their arms at me, pointing toward the exit chute. Behind them lay the electronic mat that synched with the timing chip around my ankle to record my laps. Each time I rode across it I felt like a baseball player tagging home plate. There was something between me and the mat, though: a black mesh fence stretched across the road. A barricade. One more lap. But not for me.

The race volunteer pointed toward the exit.

"You have to get off the course." The professionals were starting their race, and I'd been too slow to make it around the bend in time. If I stayed on the road, I'd be in their way.

Every other cyclist headed in the direction of the volunteer's finger, most having completed all four laps. I was in the middle of the road. If I stopped to argue I would cause a crash behind me. I pedalled to the dismount area, stopped, climbed off my bike. My legs shook, my heart knocked loudly against my chest. A lump rose in my throat, as though the adrenaline coursing through my body had gotten stuck in my oesophagus.

I hung my bike back up in its designated spot on the rack. I slid my pack off and lay it underneath my bike, Beth's photo facing skyward. It took me extra time to do this, but what did it matter at that point? I grabbed my running hat from underneath my bike. I used the Porta Potty, no toilet paper left, and made my way through the crowds of younger, faster people who started before me and were already done. Finisher's medals hung around their necks. Was I even going to get one, with my bike ride cut short? If I couldn't make it through the race, I wasn't sure how I would get through the weeks and months to follow. Was I not able to do anything for Beth, even now, even this?

Maybe a siren would go off as I crossed the finish line.

"Too slow on the bike!" the triathlon police would yell to spectators as they took me away.

I could already picture the dreaded designation next to my name on the race results sheet: DNF. Did Not Finish.

I started running.

# 1. Diagnosis

October 9th, 1997

The first time I received bad medical news, I was twenty-six years old.

I shivered in my hospital gown while I waited for the doctor to arrive, a gastroenterologist I'd never met. My boyfriend Matt was at his job a few miles away in downtown Seattle. He worked as a lab technician at a blood bank that served hospitals in a five-state region, including the one that housed the clinic where I sat.

This was my first time in this exam room, but after a year of unexplained illness and half a dozen doctors' visits the trimmings felt familiar: crinkly exam paper underneath my legs, over-bright fluorescents humming from the ceiling. Sharps container on the dull-coloured countertop, biohazard trash can by the wall-mounted blood pressure monitor. One framed print of a nature scene intended to be soothing—Mount Rainier at sunset, its glaciers painted in pastel pinks and purples.

With each doctor I saw, I had to fill out the paperwork anew. I did not yet know the habits practiced by the chronically ill. I didn't keep copies of past medical procedures or carry a notebook to record medications and their dosages. I didn't write a list of questions down ahead of time. I didn't take notes. Instead, I relied on the elephant memory I'd inherited from my mom to tell and re-tell my medical tale of woe. *Once upon a time, a twenty-six-year-old woman had a pain in her butt.*

Up to that point, I'd thought of myself as fortunate. I'd grown up in 1970s suburban Boston, the third child of a psychiatrist and a social worker who had a happy marriage. I inherited their liberal politics and desire to help disadvantaged populations. I had a boyfriend in middle school, my only dating experience until I went to college and met Matt. I rarely drank or did drugs, and didn't smoke. My biggest act of rebellion was to flaunt the advice of my prep school's college advisor and my parents and apply to a small liberal arts college in Colorado no one I knew had ever heard of, let alone attended. I got accepted and I went, declaring my first month of school that I'd never live in New England again.

\*\*\*

At the clinic, the medical assistant measured my height (holding steady at 5'2" since 1984) and weight before bringing me into the room.

"120," she announced after the scale beeped. "That's good," the doctor would tell me later. "You've maintained a healthy weight." No easy feat, considering the year I'd had.

One afternoon, the autumn before my clinic visit, I returned from a long car trip with an aching rear end. The next day I still felt pain, the sensation against my tailbone like an outlaw hunched behind a rock, waiting for his enemy to arrive. A few days later it was worse still, one man pressing the other against the rock, his lungs nearly collapsed from the pressure, a knife blade resting on his throat. Within a few months, I was pooping fifteen to twenty times a day, my stools coated with blood and mucous.

I went to urgent care, the bone and joint clinic, internal medicine. They took stool samples, blood samples, prescribed Aleve and antibiotics. On one doctor's advice,

I bought an inflatable donut pillow at the pharmacy. Finally, in October 1997, a doctor scheduled a colonoscopy. For advice on how to prepare, I called the only person I knew who'd had one—my Mom. She was the least prone to worrying of anyone in our family, and possessed a social worker's skill of listening and then dispensing wisdom in a way that made it seem like your own idea.

"Iced tea makes a good chaser," she said.

"Chaser for what?"

"For the stuff you have to drink to prep your bowels." She let out a nervous laugh. We did not talk of such intimacies, my mom and I. "It has a funny taste."

If by "funny taste" she meant a Drain-o-flavoured liquid that, years later, would make me gag simply by appearing in my line of vision on the drug store shelf, she was right.

A few days after the colonoscopy I sat in the exam room, awaiting a diagnosis. In truth, I wanted there to be something definitive wrong with me. I'd grown weary of the inconclusive diagnostic tests, the condescending tone of physicians as they dismissed my symptoms.

The doctor came in. She stood at a medium height, slightly plump, with short black hair, frameless glasses, and a raised mole above her right eyebrow that I tried not to focus on as she spoke. She wore pearl-studded earrings; a tan silk blouse peeked out from underneath her white coat.

She introduced herself, giving her first and last name. I'd never had a doctor tell me their first name before, and I lingered on it, Frances. My cousin was named Frances, and my father's sister, who died of complications from anorexia long before I was born. It was my Aunt Frances whose image I conjured in the clinic, clutching a bouquet of roses in the wedding photograph that hung on my parents' kitchen wall.

Dr Frances gave me a limp handshake, and got right to her point.

"We received the pathology report from your colonoscopy. You have Crohn's Disease."

Even though I didn't know what that meant, I felt panic course through me. I wanted to go back in time and remove my desire for a diagnosis. I didn't want one after all. Not if it had the word disease in it. Not if it made a doctor I'd just met give me such a pitying look. She began to explain what it meant to have Crohn's, but it was as though a ringing had started in my ears as soon as the word "disease" emerged from her mouth. Information came through in fragments – inflammation. Treatments improving. Chronic. Incurable. My mind snagged on this last word, then jerked forward when she asked me a question.

"Are you Jewish?"

"Half," I said. "On my Dad's side."

"Ashkenazi?"

"What?"

"The disease is more common among Ashkenazi Jews," she explained. I didn't know if that's the type of Jews we were; I'd never heard the term before. Apparently, I was the kind of Jew who doesn't know anything about being Jewish.

She asked if I had any questions. I didn't. I felt the way I did when I walked into a music store to buy CDs, where all thoughts of what I was there to purchase dissolved as soon as I walked through the metal detector at the entrance. It seemed like I should have a question, ought to say something, anything. But I was not used to asserting myself; instead, I relied on my family and friends to do it for me. Usually this method worked well, though sometimes it had dire consequences. Once I'd gone rafting with a group of inexperienced people. When we arrived at the river and I saw how high the water was, I thought it was too danger- ous to raft. I said nothing. Three of us fell out of the boat and nearly drowned.

Still, the idea of asking more of Dr Frances felt both in- appropriate and impossible, as though the chain had just derailed on the bicycle in my brain. She wrote something on her prescription pad, tore it off and handed it to me.

"This should lessen your symptoms," she said. Lessen, not eliminate. "Come back in a month and we'll see how you're doing."

She seemed a little stern, but I didn't think to be put off by this behaviour. I'd never been under ongoing care of a specialist before, and I didn't know that it was important that I like her, not just as a doctor, but as a person. We'd be seeing a lot of each other, Dr Frances and I, though I didn't understand that yet.

"You need to store this in your refrigerator," the woman behind the counter told me when I picked up the medica- tion at the hospital pharmacy one floor above the clinic. "Insert one each night at bedtime."

"Insert?"

"Yes. Into your rectum."

***

In the parking garage, I sat in my car, listening to the screech of tires and the rumble of engines as other patients entered and exited the spaces around me. I fiddled with the strap of my watch, a twenty-first birthday gift from my parents. Though it looked like fancy jewellery, with a wide piece of silver encircling its face, I wore it every day along with the baggy jeans and monochromatic t-shirts that made up the majority of my wardrobe.

In the passenger's seat a paper bag bulged with my prescription and the four-page handout of side effects, contraindications, instructions for medication administration. I should be crying, I thought. No tears came, though, just a tight, heavy feeling in my chest. I tried to let the Bad Medical News sink in, but it was like car oil pooling on the surface of a puddle. My brain couldn't make sense of the information I'd just been given, couldn't even remember most of it. This was 1997, the pre-Google era of the Internet. I couldn't instantly look up everything I needed to know about the diagnosis I'd just received. I only had single words thudding in my ears along with the roar of my heartbeat: Disease. Lifelong. Incurable.

Where was the brochure I was supposed to be handed, bolstering me with facts? Therapies were improving all the time; there were support groups I could join. Over a million people in the United States suffered from Crohn's or its cousin illness, ulcerative colitis, many of them young people like me. My Crohn's seemed to be limited to my rectum, but the disease could affect any portion of the digestive tract, mouth to anus. Patients sometimes experienced "flare ups," a worsening of symptoms for a distinct period of time.

But I didn't know any of this yet. It felt as if there was one true thing, which was that this was not supposed to be my fate. Bad things did not happen to me. I was twenty-six years old. Every single person I knew under forty was in their prime of health. The previous summer some friends from Colorado stayed in our apartment on their way to summit Mount Rainier. It felt like a cruel contrast, the three of them going to rent climbing gear while I stayed home with the phone to my ear, on hold while the nurse looked up my latest test result. This would be my vantage point now, navigating adulthood from the waiting room chair instead of the mountain top.

Being ill for the past year had made me feel lonely, and the prospect of living the rest of my life with a chronic illness lonelier still. It was as though all my life up to that point I'd been walking a trail through the woods with a group of family and friends. We sang songs and paused to observe mushrooms and wildflowers, the way the leaves and branches above us were shot with sunlight. The route was obvious, signalled by bright yellow blazes painted on the trunks of the trees that lined the path. Sitting in the hospital garage, though, it seemed to me that my trail had veered left, away from the others. No more markers, no more companions. The way ahead was brambled and dark.

I needed to talk to someone, immediately. It was late afternoon. Matt worked the swing shift, and calls were difficult to take at the lab, so phoning him was out. My college friends Amy and Penny, to whom I confided everything, lived in different states and would also still be at work. I could call my best friend in Seattle, Beth, but I'd rather tell her in person. My sister in New York was probably eager for a distraction. She was a week past her due date for her first child, no doubt pacing the apartment double-checking the contents of the duffel bag she'd bring to the hospital. My brother, in his first year of medical school, would surely have some up-to-date wisdom to pass along.

I decided on my parents back in Massachusetts. They'd be home from work by now, my mom preparing dinner while she listened to All Things Considered, a glass of wine on the counter next to the cutting board. My father, in his study, would be responding to emails while he drank a Diet Coke. I took a shallow breath. I started my car, exited the garage, and pointed towards home.

The apartment I shared with Matt sat twenty blocks from the clinic, and 3,060 miles from my childhood home in Massachusetts. My parents moved into the house a few months before I was born and still lived there twenty-seven years later. The western-most edge of Interstate 90 began a few miles from my home in Seattle and ended approximately the same distance from my parents' house.

"One road from my house to yours," I joked to my mom over the phone when I made the discovery. Then it had felt true, a thick rope that stretched from one side of the country to the other, shrinking the distance between us much the same way the telephone line did. Nonstop flights departed Seattle for Boston every day, and I could travel from one house to the other in less than six hours. But as I exited the hospital parking garage and drove past the university campus, it was my childhood home I longed for. For the first time since arriving in Seattle, I was overcome by a wave of homesickness so strong my vision blurred for a moment.

I'd moved to Seattle with Matt two years earlier intent on eliminating poverty. It was a goal I'd had in mind since high school when I interned at a child care centre for abused and neglected infants and toddlers. I continued along my public service path by spending every Tuesday afternoon in college tutoring kids at the Red Cross homeless shelter a few miles from campus. After graduation I spent four months in Kathmandu working for a Nepali women's rights organization.

My role model was my grandmother, who as one of the first female attorneys in the country had dedicated her career to helping disadvantaged people. Her briefcase was a 1960s-style rainbow-striped Technicolour affair. Grey-haired and 5'3," she would walk calmly down the courtroom aisle and set her briefcase down on the counsel table with a confident thwap. I wanted to be her.

***

I pulled up to a red light and rolled down my window. It was early October and the maples and dogwoods that lined the university campus were just beginning to change into their autumn wardrobes. On either side of the boulevard students and faculty transported themselves from building to building by foot, bicycle, skateboard. To my left, Lake Union appeared to be painted in gunmetal with a matte finish, churning as the wind picked up. To my right, the Burke-Gilman, a rail-trail that bisected campus and continued north for some twenty miles. I jogged on the Burke-Gilman regularly, crossing the drawbridge near our apartment to run along the path. I hadn't gone running in months, though. I'd been too sick and in too much pain. Maybe the medication would help me feel well enough to resume running. Did people with Crohn's Disease exercise, I wondered?

I parked in front of our apartment and sat in my car for a moment before gathering my prescription and my backpack from work. Inside the house I kicked off my shoes and shucked my rain jacket, hanging it on the over-full coat tree. I flicked on light switches and walked straight to the phone, eager to hear my parents' voices and share my news. My father, Harvard-educated in English Literature and medicine, would surely have something erudite to say. The words "Crohn's Disease" had barely escaped my mouth before he gave his response.

"Oh, shit."

# 2. From the Centennial State to the Land of the Chronically Ill

Prior to the diagnosis, before the Before, and way before the After, there was the college romance. When Matt and I met during our first semester at Colorado College, I was the shy and unassertive one. We lived two floors apart in our all-freshman dorm, where I viewed him as part of the boisterous group of guys who lived in his hall. Sophomore year, our groups of friends merged and I had my first conversations with Matt; my opinion of him changed. He seemed interesting and smart. And cute. He wore his red hair in a tidy ponytail that framed his slender, high-cheekboned face. At six-foot-two inches he slouched—to remain at the same height as his best friends in high school, he said—and his shoulders sloped at steep angles. I liked looking at his arms, the ropy veins and sprinkling of moles covered in a thin layer of strawberry-blonde hair.

One winter night during our sophomore year, I encountered Matt in his dorm lounge and we decided to go to 7-11 for a midnight snack. We walked diagonally across campus, the thin layer of snow on the quad crunching under our shoes. Behind the student centre we could make out the faint outline of Pike's Peak and the surrounding foothills, darker shapes backgrounded by an indigo sky. It was the first time I'd ever been alone with Matt. My heart thrummed. Does this count as a date? I wondered. Did he want to be my boyfriend?

My boyfriend. The words sounded strange inside my head. I could tick off my romantic interludes on one hand: a boyfriend for the entirety of sixth grade, and a couple of one-night fumblings with boys during my first year of college. Matt had turned twenty the previous month; I was nineteen. If we became a couple, we'd do our growing up together. Either that or we'd grow in different directions, and the relationship would fail. I'd seen it happen to friends, the melodramatic breakups or the fizzling connections. The awkward encounters waiting in the keg line at a party, the old boyfriend standing shoulder-to-shoulder with a different girl.

If Matt felt nervous too, he didn't show it. He pointed out the course of his new favourite sport, Frisbee golf. Extending his arm into the darkness, he pointed towards the bronze statue of a school trustee that stood in front of the library.

"Ten points if you hit Charles Tutt's head."

At 7-11, under the fluorescent lights, we contemplated our options. We rejected beef-and-cheese burritos, Snickers bars, microwave popcorn, before settling on our snack: a large bag of Cool Ranch Doritos, and two sixteen-ounce bottles of Sprite. We returned to Matt's dorm and climbed two flights of stairs. Everything in his room sat on the floor: mattress, stereo, overstuffed red laundry bag. We leaned against his unmade bed, our fingers coated with Dorito essence as we listened to Fishbone and Michael Hedges. Matt showed me his Ronald Reagan shadow puppet trick on a section of blank wall. We talked and talked through several albums. Sometime after three a.m. he finally turned to me.

"Can I kiss you?"

We'd been a couple ever since. It wasn't long before I gained a little self-confidence and a sense of adventure. After graduation, I changed locations almost as often as I changed my sheets: a ski resort town, Denver, ski town, Nepal. I spent several months working in Kathmandu and travelling before I returned to Matt. While I spent two years zigzagging around Colorado and Asia, Matt lived with friends in the ski town, working at a paint and decorating store and perfecting his telemark turns. I wrote long letters from Nepal on air mail stationary and he sent short ones back via fax machine. *Justin drove your car into a ditch, but no damage. Miss and love you always.* He sounded like he thought I wasn't coming back.

But I did come back, slightly shrunken from near-constant intestinal illness and ready to stay put. At some previous and un-definable point in time I'd become the one who called the shots. I wasn't interested in staying in the ski town.

"Let's move to a city," I said.

"Okay," Matt said. He was mild-mannered and agreeable, products, he told me, of growing up in Iowa. "We Midwesterners are an easy-going bunch." My mom, raised in Cleveland, certainly exemplified that style; she was the most relaxed person I knew and had brought up three children without ever raising her voice. I was turning out to be like my father, a worrier and an over-thinker. But I liked planning a future with Matt. On hikes we discussed our options. San Francisco. Washington, D.C. We had friends in both places, and had visited each city as children, before we met.

"How about Seattle?" I asked. Seattle sat on the water, a feature I'd missed since leaving Boston, and near the mountains, which we'd both grown to love. There was a university, in case we wanted more schooling. There would be jobs and apartments aplenty, so we could arrive in town with neither secured.

"But I've never been there," Matt said. "We don't know anyone."

"We know two people," I said, naming classmates who were distant friends. We'd both entered college knowing no one, I pointed out. "This time, we have each other."

"That's true," Matt said. "Seattle sounds cool. Should I join a grunge band?"

Just like that, it was decided. I felt excited at the uncharted territory of living together, just the two of us. Up to that point we'd spent our entire relationship as part of a larger group. Outside of the bedroom, we rarely spent time alone. Meals, ski days, outings to the bar always took place with some combination of friends. I imagined candlelit dinners for two at the dining room table we planned to bring with us to Seattle, formerly used as a ski-tuning surface by a local rental shop. I envisioned exploring Washington's evergreen-covered mountains together, sleeping in the turquoise backpacking tent Matt bought when he joined the college outdoor recreation club.

\*\*\*

After I got sick, the actual scenes were decidedly less romantic—we walked to the pharmacy together to pick up my prescriptions, then ate Thai takeout on TV trays in front of the television. Before my illness, it felt like we'd been play-acting at being grownups. Our first year in Seattle, our explorations of the city and surrounding natural beauty left me feeling almost tipsy. But it was as though my

Crohn's diagnosis had sobered us up. We were grown-ups too soon, dealing with an adult-sized problem before we were ready.

Crohn's was my biggest problem, but it wasn't my only problem. With everyone but Matt, I was timid. These hadn't been obstacles when I was healthy, but now that I would be spending a lot of time at the doctor's office, they would be liabilities. As a young woman, if I didn't speak up, my symptoms and concerns would be glossed over by my doctors. I would need to become my own advocate.

No one told me this. If there was a guide to being a patient, I didn't know of its existence. My usual methods—read about the issue, talk to family and friends—yielded little useful information. Everyone was supportive, but I was a pioneer in the Land of the Chronically Ill.

In the month following my diagnosis, I continued to take the nightly steroid suppositories, as well as an oral medication. My stools were now absent of blood and mucous. The pain continued, but with less intensity; I no longer required the donut pillow at work. I pooped at least ten times a day, less than before, but still too often.

If the shift in my physical symptoms seemed moderate, they became eclipsed by the dramatic change in my outlook. Before Crohn's, I felt frustrated by my protracted illness and motivated to find a cure. After the diagnosis, though, I felt deflated. Crohn's was incurable. Crohn's lasted forever. How was I going to get through it?

I realized that I would have to endure my chronic condition the way I'd managed everything else: by being good. I'd been a good daughter, taking the straight-laced path in the wake of my sister's rebellious adolescence. I'd been a good student, friend, girlfriend. And now I would be a good patient. I took my medications dutifully, and followed all my doctor's instructions to the letter. My brother, immersed in his medical school coursework, had advice. My father, several years past his med school days, had more. I took all their suggestions, just as I had my entire life. And then one day, at the very wrong moment, I'd had enough.

My father called one evening with a recommendation from Bob, one of his closest friends from college and medical school.

"Bob knows a gastroenterologist in Seattle," my father told me. "He was a year behind us in school. I don't remember him." He was the head of a clinic associated with one of the large hospitals, though not the one where I was getting treatment. "Bob can put you in touch with him if you like."

"I like my doctor," I said. This was true and not true. She'd treated Crohn's patients for years, and seemed like a good doctor who knew what she was talking about. I found her manner condescending, though. She had a stand-offish tone that, years later, made me wonder if she preferred the research part of her job to patient care. But the clinic had a good reputation, part of a state-of-the-art hospital with access to the latest treatments.

I chose the clinic for reasons that made sense to a twenty-six-year-old who'd never had a serious illness: It was close to our apartment and covered by my insurance. When my first symptoms—the tailbone pain—cropped up, I didn't have a primary care physician. I went to urgent care hoping they'd prescribe some heavy-duty pain reliever and send me on my way. Instead, they took an x-ray and referred me to the bone and joint clinic. From there I bounced to a general practitioner, who took some stool samples and tried a few rounds of antibiotics before sending me to a specialist. The GI clinic was where the buck stopped, and my doctor seemed as well qualified as anyone else would be to take care of me.

Throughout our lives my father's well-connected status had yielded gifts for his children—front row seats to the Eric Clapton concert when I was in high school, or a space for my sister in her college dorm even though they were purportedly full. We had to earn the important things— jobs and school admissions—on our own. It was his way of taking care of us, a character trait I saw as generous from the vantage point of older adulthood.

In those early years in Seattle, though, I wanted to feel I'd made choices that were both wise and my own. I'd opted to settle on the west coast, not the choice my parents would have made for me. Now I was choosing to stay with the doctor I'd found. No matter that the one my father knew was one of the top gastroenterologists in Seattle, and likely had a long waitlist I could hop with a phone call from Bob. Maybe my father was simply encouraging me to shop around, that I didn't have to stick with someone I didn't love. But I didn't see it that way. I saw it as judgment. His choice right, my choice wrong.

"She's a good doctor." I told my Dad. "Tell Bob thanks anyway."

\*\*\*

Our first Christmas in Seattle, two months after my diagnosis, I stood in our kitchen making dinner with Matt. We played our usual roles: Matt at the stove, stirring and seasoning, me at the counter slicing and dicing. Our closest local friends, Beth and Kevin, were coming for dinner. They were vegetarians, so I'd planned a menu adapted from the holiday issue of *Martha Stewart Living*: pumpkin soup served in miniature pumpkins, honey-glazed carrots, wilted chard salad. A loaf of crusty bread from the neighbourhood bakery sat on the counter, waiting to be warmed. The night before I'd made apple pie—my mom's recipe, not Martha's—and a pint of Ben & Jerry's World's Best Vanilla sat in the freezer. The fridge held our lunch leftovers: dips and salads from the deli at the overpriced co-op grocery store. All the delicacies for the holiday. It had been that way my entire life.

In my family, food stood in place of religion. We had two refrigerators perpetually crammed with grapes in a ceramic colander, leftover lasagne, half-full jars of spaghetti sauce, three different kinds of mustard. My favourite childhood chore was unloading the food delivered from the local grocery store. While the delivery driver shot baskets with my brother in our driveway, I'd dart around the kitchen, using my blossoming organizational skills to find a space on the shelves for each item.

How soul-crushing, then, to be diagnosed with a disease that would forever impact my food choices and my digestion. In 1997, the idea of eliminating foods to control intestinal distress was still avant-garde, even in a mecca of alternative medicine like Seattle. I performed my own experiments, and came up with an anti-shopping list of foods to avoid: beans, lettuce, corn, nuts. Tomatoes proved difficult to digest, more so to give up, so I kept eating them.

Matt opened the oven door to check on the roasting pumpkins. He poked one with a fork.

"Five more minutes," he said.

"I'll set the table," I said. Matt moved from the stove to step in front of me as I headed to the dining room, wrapping his arm around my waist and dipping me, ballroom-dance style. He righted me, then bent down for a kiss. I kissed him back, then pulled away when he started to move his hands down my back.

"Beth and Kevin will be here any minute," I said in a mock-scolding tone. "Besides, didn't you get enough earlier?" We'd had sex that afternoon, the time of day when my intestines were their quietest and intercourse held its highest appeal for me. Not that it did very often in those days. This made me different from other women my age, or so I assumed. In college, my friends and I talked openly about sex. But in Seattle, the rules were different, or maybe I was. I felt more private about my relationship with Matt than I had back in Colorado. All couples go through fallow periods, I told myself. They must. But wasn't it a little early in life to lose my libido? We weren't even thirty yet.

I went into the dining room and dug placemats out of the built-in hutch that covered one wall. The apartment took up the main floor of a two-story Craftsman house. Our neighbourhood was covered in turn-of-the-century homes like this one, houses originally built for employees of the Seattle Lighting Company who worked at the coal gasification plant down the hill on Lake Union. The house was draughty, with lead pipes, knob-and-tube wiring, and asbestos siding. We loved it for its hardwood floors and light-filled living room. Our cat had already made a habit of climbing into the unlit fire place and up the chimney's interior, emerging in the upstairs neighbour's living room sooty and proud of his cleverness.

As I set placemats on the table, the doorbell rang. I walked through the living room, pausing to turn down the volume on the *Ella's Swingin' Christmas* CD before I opened the door. Beth and Kevin stood on our porch. He held a six-pack of beer and she held a flat present wrapped in plain brown paper—a recycled grocery bag, her signature—and a bright red bow.

"Ho, ho, ho!" Beth said, stepping into our entryway to wrap me in a hug.

"Merry Christmas!" I said, hugging them both.

"Pardon our moisture," Beth said as they removed their shoes and shed rain-covered jackets. "We just walked around Green Lake. We had the place to ourselves." She beamed. Beth was always pleased when she could pursue unpopulated activities in the city.

"Wet but happy," I said. Their cheeks were flushed and Beth's eyes caught the light from the fixture above our heads. "Matt's in the kitchen," I said, and Kevin headed to the back of the apartment, the six-pack still in his hand. Beth stepped into the living room and put the present under the Christmas tree.

"For later," she said. "What can I do?"

"Help me set the table?" We went into the dining room, Beth chattering about her visit to her aunt and uncle's house the night before as I handed her napkins, silverware, glasses. I set a stack of plates on the table, ivory-coloured with fat yellow birds painted onto their centres.

"Wow," Beth said. "The good china."

"The Queensbird collection," I said, waving my hand in a little flourish.

"Fancy. Is it new?"

"New and old," I said. "Some of the pieces were my grandmother's wedding china." The rest, I explained, were part of my sister's registry from her wedding five years before. After the wedding she and her husband decided they didn't want it. Ever since, the dishes had sat in my parents' storage room, unused, until the month before when, while Matt and I visited for Thanksgiving, my mom had offered them to me.

"Why now?" Beth said. She widened her eyes in mock

horror. "Is there something you haven't told me? You're getting married?"

"No," I said, laughing to cover the lurch in my stomach. "My mom was just tired of them sitting around unused."

That was a partial truth. My mom had also been lamenting our lack of dishes since we'd moved to Seattle. Before the Queensbird arrived, we had a total of six plates, four bought at Goodwill, two stolen from our college dining hall. But there was something I wasn't telling Beth about marriage, something I hadn't told anyone. Thinking of it as we set the table, I had to turn away from Beth so that she wouldn't see my flushed face or hear my hammering heart.

It had happened in our first apartment, a few months after we moved to Seattle. Matt and I were watching *E.R.*, a favourite show before my illness and after. A commercial came on. Matt picked up the remote, lowered the volume, and turned to me.

"Will you marry me?" he said. I thought he was kidding, and I laughed. His face fell. He was serious. Shit.

"Um," I stalled.

It wasn't that I didn't want to marry Matt. I did. Just not right then. None of our friends were married, and I didn't want to be that kind of trendsetter. Moving somewhere together had been the biggest commitment I felt ready to make. It would be years before we'd be ready to have kids, or discussions about the rest of our lives. That was how I felt, anyway.

"Not right now?" I said it like a question. There was a silence, but not the comfortable kind between two people who know each other intimately. We watched the rest of the episode without speaking. I felt embarrassed, as though someone had been there to witness Matt's question and my refusal. A proposal while watching television? It didn't fit the image I'd held in my head since childhood of that milestone moment.

Sometime later, I had a proposal of my own: "Let's wait."

\*\*\*

Where does assertive give way to bossy and controlling? Some time in our past I had crossed that line with Matt, though I wouldn't notice until years later. Maybe I had assertiveness inside me that I only felt safe to demonstrate with him. But it was like the water stored in a fire hydrant; it couldn't come out in a moderate quantity. It never occurred to me to worry about whether or not Matt would stay with me. I took it as a given.

Some men would have fled when their girlfriends shat blood and mucous or required nightly steroid suppositories. Not Matt. He didn't get grossed out. He didn't alter his behaviour. He stayed right by my side. I should have married him right then, for that reason alone. But I felt too worn-down to consider marriage or a wedding. I didn't feel celebratory. I felt as though I was perpetually at the tail-end of a flu I couldn't quite shake.

That Christmas night, though, I felt okay. By the time Beth and I had finished setting the table, dinner was ready. The four of us bustled around the kitchen, ladling soup into the little roasted sugar pumpkins and carrying vegetable-filled serving bowls to the table. Soon everything was in the dining room and we sat down.

I raised my cider-filled wine glass to make a toast and the other three lifted their beers. I hesitated. Except for when I lived in Nepal, this was my only Christmas not spent at my parents' house. My father always made the toast, quoting the last line in A Christmas Carol, "God bless us, everyone."

It was a tribute to Dickens, one of my father's favourite authors, and had long since lost any religious connotations
for our family. But still, it was too much God for Catholic-
turned-atheist Beth. She didn't even like to say "bless you"
after someone sneezed. Instead, she said the Spanish word
for health, which is also what you say in Spanish when you
toast. So that was my toast. "*Salud.*"

"*Salud,*" everyone chorused. We clinked our glasses together. We laughed. And then we ate.

# 3. Replicas

I met Beth two months after I moved to Seattle, on my first day of work. I'd been hired by a large social service agency to create a family centre that would be housed down the hall from the agency's food bank. The family centre would hold free classes for clients and other members of the community on topics like budgeting, cooking, parenting, English as a Second Language. I would be part of VISTA, a national service program that was a domestic version of the Peace Corps.

A few days before I started at the agency, I travelled to a Seattle suburb to attend a state-wide VISTA training. The retreat centre where we spent three days had a swimming pool. One evening, despite the crowd in the water and the lack of lane lines, I attempted to swim laps. Once my goggles fogged over, the result was inevitable: a head-on collision with another swimmer. My nose bled on impact, and by morning I had a pronounced black eye.

The following Monday the department director at the agency greeted me in the lobby with a warm smile and a booming hello. His grin faded as he examined my face.

"Should I ask?" he said, pointing to my eye. I told the swimming pool story and he worked it into my introductions as we went from office to office, each a small room jutting out to the right of a long corridor. A tall, broad-torsoed man with a red beard he kept well-trimmed, he had to walk in front of me so we could both fit down the narrow hall.

"This is Janet," he would say. "She's our new VISTA. Another VISTA gave her a black eye during their training session." I got looks of pity, or laughter if I laughed. Most of my new co-workers looked like me: white women in their twenties. The director was talkative, and it took us a long time to make our way down the hall. Two doors up from the conference room, a redheaded woman sat at a desk, her back to the open door of her office. She swiveled in her chair when we knocked, then stood when she saw us.

"Hi!" she said in a tone of familiarity, like we were old friends. This was her in-person greeting, I would learn later, a drawn-out, two syllable hi-i.

"This is Beth," the director told me, then delivered his lines.

"*That's* how you're introducing her?" Beth said.

"I didn't want people to get the wrong idea," he said defensively. "Start slipping her brochures for our women's shelter program." Beth, a former domestic violence counsellor, narrowed her eyes at him. Then she turned to me, and smiled.

"It's really nice to meet you." she said, reaching out to shake my hand. She wore cropped khakis and a short-sleeved button-down. Her thick hair, a shade more orange than Matt's, hung past her shoulders. I'd soon learn that she changed hairstyles frequently—cutting it short, growing it out, tying it into a ponytail during a staff meeting and then removing the hair band a few minutes later.

A brightness extended from her smile outward, as though the light above her head was a theatre stage light instead of a buzzing fluorescent. Her blue eyes sparkled like she couldn't wait to see what would happen next. She smirked, a friend sharing an inside joke.

"Don't pay any attention to him," She said as she gestured towards the department director, her boss' boss. "He doesn't know anything."

"It's true," the department director said, smiling at Beth like a proud father. "That's why I hire such great people, to do my thinking for me." The three of us laughed and I watched Beth, thinking, she's brave. It wasn't long before I returned to her desk, or she to mine, to sit and talk. Or I'd lean in the door of her office, asking, "is it lunchtime yet?"

\*\*\*

Two major events marked Beth's childhood: a move from Chicago to Seattle when she was ten, and the death of her mom from brain cancer when Beth was sixteen. She rarely spoke about her mom's death, but it seemed to have shaped her adult self. Despite her light-bulb personality, Beth had a wide cynical streak. Perhaps that came with the territory of losing a parent when you were a teenager, old enough to have memories of happiness ground to a halt by disease and death. After her mom was gone, and even after her father remarried, Beth took on a caretaker role for her two younger brothers. She fit into the mother hen role naturally, standing up to their would-be aggressors on the school playground and advocating for a more generous dessert policy at home.

Even though we were only four months apart in age, Beth seemed older than me, and wiser. She behaved towards me the way my older sister did, giving her opinion about how I should act with a fervency that left no room to do anything except obey. Beth stood up for herself and spoke her mind, two traits I lacked. In choosing her as my friend I employed a strategy I'd used since my ultra-shy childhood: find an extrovert and stick close to her. I had to be careful, though, not to mimic her gestures too closely, or I might botch it. I'd learnt at an early age that there were limits to how well or how long you could pretend to be someone you're not.

The first time I hurt another girl was in the swimming pool at summer camp when I was six. During free swim at the end of lessons I usually hovered on the pool deck, hesitant, like a teen driver afraid to merge into traffic. Then I met Jody. She'd skipped Kindergarten and wore her curly hair short, Little Orphan Annie style, and talked and chewed gum constantly.

One day when the whistle blew for free swim, Jody grabbed my hand and we ran together, laughing. What a relief not to linger at the edge of the pool, worrying. I did not look before I leapt. I just jumped. Another girl was already in the water, practicing her back float. How peaceful she must have felt in the moment before my feet hit her stomach.

In two breast strokes I was at the ladder, scrambling up, hoping a swift exit from the pool would somehow undo my actions. Nearby, the swim coach turned and blew his whistle, his extended arm and finger pointed at me.

"Watch where you're jumping!" he yelled while a counsellor helped the girl. "No running on the pool deck." My eyes filled. I'd never before been scolded by a stranger. Walking back from the pool, I saw the girl vomiting onto the grass. I can still picture her bathing suit: a blue-and-red lattice pattern with a frilly skirt at the waist.

*** 

By the time I met Beth I'd learnt that it worked better if my outgoing friends made their grand gestures on their own while I watched. Beth wouldn't have taken well to a close imitation anyway. She was her own person, strident in her beliefs even if they didn't match those around her. I'd never met anyone my age with such strong convictions about her future.

"People assume that because I work with moms and babies, I want kids of my own," she told me shortly after we met. "I don't. My mind is made up." No children? The idea was foreign and the opposite of how I felt. I was surprised by the finality of her statement. As I got to know her better, I learnt that Beth did not make decisions with ease. Most actions—from choosing the right clothes to pack for a long trip to who to vote for in an upcoming election – required deliberation. She'd often call me or come into my office for a consultation, giving a long list of pros and cons before asking my opinion.

Not that she did not have one of her own. She had strong views about everything, and a long list of favourite items: green tea ice cream, Gruyere cheese, a chocolate-coated, chopstick-shaped cookie called Pocky. Several stuffed zebras—her favourite animal—dotted the bookshelves around the tiny house three blocks from our office that she and Kevin shared. Most of their other decorations were art pieces friends had made or items Beth had bought while travelling in Latin America. Their house had an uncluttered feel—Ikea furniture, small television, the slimmest model stereo available. Still, there were splashes of style: a purple couch that Beth bought from a co-worker for fifty dollars, a lichen-coloured Zen alarm clock that made a gentle chime like a gong at a Tibetan monastery.

One day while standing in her living room, Beth surprised me with an announcement.

"I've decided to collect pewter replicas." A few months before, she and Kevin had taken a road trip to Chicago to attend a wedding. On the way there and back they'd detoured to the most Americana places they could find—Mount Rushmore, Wall Drug, the world's largest ball of twine in Cawker City, Kansas. While browsing the gift shops, Beth had delighted in learning about people who collected the same kind of souvenir from every tourist attraction—bells, spoons, coffee mugs.

"Pewter replicas are harder to find," Beth told me, picking up the one she'd bought at her favourite site, the Corn Palace in South Dakota. She cradled it in her palm for a moment like a hamster she'd just brought home from the pet store, then handed it to me. It was impressive, a sort of a Taj Mahal with tiny kernel-shaped beads comprising the pillars and minarets.

"It gets redecorated every year," Beth said as I handed the replica back to her and she returned it to its spot on the bookshelf. "They use thirteen different shades of corn, and nail it up ear by ear. Isn't that amazing?"

She was pleased by the smallest things, and thus made me eager to please her. I'd begun to notice a trait in myself that I didn't like but couldn't control—the need to be not just a friend, but an *important* friend. To me this meant solving some kind of problem no one else could solve—connecting someone with a great car mechanic or fixing a faucet that had leaked for years. Since I was new to the city, and not the least bit handy, the services I could offer were harder to conjure. But then Beth provided me with one.

"Next time you go somewhere touristy, will you look for replicas?"

Matt and I went to Colorado to ski in the town where we'd lived before moving to Seattle. While getting an *après-ski* snack one day I said I wanted to go into F.M. Light and Sons, the most touristy of the tourist shops.

"I need to find a pewter replica for Beth," I told Matt. I searched every corner of the store, which was full of anything you might need to outfit a cowboy—ten-gallon hats, pearl-buttoned plaid shirts, spurs, chaps—but no replicas.

"It's just a tacky pewter thing," Matt said when I emerged from the store looking dejected. "Why do you care so much?"

Why *did* I care? I couldn't say. I only knew that Beth's attention was like that theatre light that seemed to hover above her head was shining on me. It felt nice, that focus, and different from the way most of my friendships in Seattle seemed to work, with a barrier between me and the other person you could almost reach out and touch. With Beth it was more like the connection I felt with my friends from my pre-Seattle life, like there was an invisible thread that connected us.

But how strong was that thread? Would it hold under pressure, or would some event sever it, a blunder made in a moment of clumsiness? Beth would not be the one to blame. Her insights about people and relationships seemed generated from a long and storied past, as though the Beth we knew was the reincarnation of a less self-assured person. She had life figured out, it seemed to me, and my best strategy would be to stay close in hopes that some of the grace with which she moved about the world might rub off on me.

If a problem lay ahead, then, surely I would be the cause of it. I needed to be careful not to mess anything up. I wouldn't allow myself to be the source of any pain.

# 4. Abscess

Most of the time, I could focus on friendships, on Matt, on my job. Sometimes, though, the Crohn's symptoms would take over. In March I experienced my first disease complication: a flare-up. My pain and bowel movements increased suddenly, and the medication didn't help. Dr Frances performed a sigmoidoscopy, a procedure in which she inserted a small scope into my rectum, displaying the inside of my colon on a colour monitor in the exam room. I lay on the exam table in a fetal position, cramping from the air blown up my anus to allow the scope interior access.

"What's that?" I asked, gesturing to an angry red lump on the screen.

"That's just a polyp," Dr Frances said. "Lots of people have those. It's unrelated to your Crohn's." The exam didn't reveal anything conclusive, so she ordered at CT scan for a Friday afternoon. I wouldn't be allowed to eat anything until late afternoon, a state that sounded worse to me than the scan itself.

"It's a routine procedure, not as uncomfortable as the sigmoidoscopy," Dr Frances said, smiling her mouth-only smile. "I'll call you with the results."

My third bite of dinner, my only food all day, had been on its way to my mouth when the phone rang.

"You have an abscess," Dr Frances said, breathless, like she'd read the radiology report and run up a flight of stairs to call me. I thought I detected a note of excitement in her voice: finally my mild, hard-to-treat Crohn's Disease was asserting itself in some identifiable way.

"You need to go to the hospital. Immediately."

Landing in the E.R. at the age of twenty-six would have terrified me if Matt hadn't been there. During a crisis, he behaved like I imagined a Buddhist monk at the scene of a car accident would act. I'm certain my pulse slowed as we sat opposite one another, me in the bed in a curtained-off area and Matt in a vinyl-cushioned chair.

Down the emergency room hall, machines beeped and gurney wheels bumped along the scratched linoleum. The smell of disinfectant covered every other scent I imagined might be present at any given time: vomit, faeces, blood, booze.

In order to stay warm, I'd put my jeans back on underneath my hospital gown like a three-year-old who wanted to wear pants and a twirly dress to school. After four failed attempts to find a good vein in my arm, the nurse inserted a port into the back of my hand where an IV would be placed when I went upstairs for surgery. If I went upstairs.

"I thought it would be busier," I said.

"I thought it would be faster," Matt said.

"We should have brought something to read."

"I'm hungry."

"I'm starving."

"I bet." He paused, then reached over to rub my leg. "I hope you don't have to have surgery."

"Me too."

Two hours after we arrived, the surgical resident stood in the curtained-off area, peering at my CT scan on the film reader.

"I *guess* that's an abscess," he said. He was handsome: short, early thirties, with a shaved head and frameless glasses. He turned to me, taking in my gown-and-jeans ensemble, my arms crossed for warmth.

"You look too good to be here." It sounded like a pick-up line, and I blushed. But it wasn't flattery, it was doctor-speak. He meant: I'm not much older than you, but I've been through four years of medical school, and six years of residency, and now I'm the Chief Surgical Resident of a busy urban hospital and in my experience when someone needs surgery they look like they need it, if you know what I mean. You are too far from death's door. You don't even have a fever, for Pete's sake.

I decided right then that I liked the resident better than my regular doctor. In my growing survey of medical professionals, I'd begun to notice a trend. The younger the doctor, the more he or she listened to me. They asked questions and in their responses to my own, conveyed both confidence and a willingness to admit when they didn't know the answer. They seemed more like peers with special knowledge than experts making a distant pronouncement. More like my brother, in other words, our family doctor-in-training. In talking to people like my brother, I felt more comfortable giving my opinion.

"I don't feel like I need emergency surgery," I said.

"You don't," the resident said as he pulled my scan off the film reader and turned back to me. "We can track the abscess through weekly CT scans. I'm giving you antibiotics and sending you home."

The next week I sat in the radiology department waiting room, drinking oral contrast from a wax paper cup. If you drank it slowly, as I did, the wax disintegrated, tiny flakes like fish food floating on the surface of the yellowed liquid. They mixed it with Crystal Light to sweeten it; I thought it tasted like Crystal Light long past its sell-by date.

Of the substances I'd had to consume to prepare my intestines for medical procedures, oral contrast ranked in the middle, taste-wise. Slightly worse than the milkshake-like Barium, far better than Phosphosoda, the near-toxic liquid I had to drink before my colonoscopy. Phosphosoda tasted like bathroom cleanser, and required a Root Beer chaser. It made me sputter and gag and come close to vomiting. If I had to drink something in front of an audience of other waiting-room sitters I'd choose oral contrast over Phosphosoda any day.

By my third scan, they knew to get their best vein-finder when they called me back to the scanner room. One nurse had written *difficult stick* on my chart. I resented the adjectives used to describe me, *pleasant twenty-six-year-old*, or the way the specialists signed their notes: *thank you for referring this interesting patient to us.* If you have a chronic medical problem, for goodness sakes don't be boring, or unpleasant, or possess tiny veins.

While waiting in the hallway for my fourth scan, I saw a classmate from the Spanish class I took on Monday evenings at the university extension.

"*Hola, doctora,*" I almost called out, a reflex, but then I stopped myself. What would I say after that? That I had an abscess that may or may not have been shrinking in size, depending on which radiologist read the scan? That the antibiotics they'd had me on all month had given me a yeast infection? That in addition to the oral contrast I drank ahead of time, during the scan I had contrast running through an IV into my arm, and through an enema bag into my rectum? That no one, including me, had raised concern about the larger problem I might have—cancer—

if I went through the scanner too many more times? It didn't matter. My classmate, deep in conversation with another doctor, did not notice the half-naked patient sitting in the corridor. He walked right past.

At my follow-up appointment six weeks after my E.R. visit I lay on the exam table while the shaved-head resident felt my abdomen for lumps.

"Finish this round of antibiotics," he said, "and then you're done. No more scans."

"Why hasn't the abscess gone away?" I asked.

"I don't know. But it's not getting bigger. We shouldn't keep making you come back here. Go on and live your life."

He reached out his hand and I put mine in his, thinking he meant to shake it. I was still lying down. Instead of shaking my hand, he pulled on it until I was sitting up. Helping me, not because I was pleasant or a difficult stick or because I did or did not have an abscess, but just because. I'd never had a doctor do that before, and it felt oddly personal, this extending of his arm, like we were teammates and I'd fallen on the soccer field. Maybe we'd all meet for beers later and laugh about the game, or the abscess, or the fact that I'd had so many scans that month it was a wonder I didn't glow in the dark.

He reached his hand out again, and this time shook mine.

"Good luck," he said, and left the exam room. He pulled the door closed slowly, marking his exit with a faint click of the latch. I got dressed and placed the hospital gown unfolded on top of the wrinkled exam paper. I left the door ajar. Before I'd rounded the corner I could hear the medical assistant crumpling the used paper and smoothing a fresh sheet across the table as she readied the room for the next patient.

# 5. The Princess Bride

Life with a chronic illness, it seemed, was an obstacle-filled endurance race. I'd overcome one barrier, then brace myself for the next. I went to bed each night not knowing how I'd feel when I awoke. The uncertainty and inability to plan drove me crazy. I developed a jaw disorder from grinding my teeth in my sleep.

In the spring of 1998, several months after my diagnosis, Beth made an announcement that threw me off-course once again. She and Kevin were moving to Ecuador. They'd lined up jobs, housing, visas, passports.

"For a year, give or take," Beth said. "We might come back to Seattle, we might not. The future is uncertain." She grinned. She enjoyed the anticipation of the unmapped journey, craved it even. In this way, we were opposites.

"Wow," I said, forcing a smile back. "You're brave." I said other things too: *How exciting! What an adventure you'll have!* Wasn't this what you said when one of your best friends realized her dream of living and working abroad? Not the truth: I'm jealous. I'm hurt.

The envy came from the fact that I'd once been that person, the one who craved that kind of adventure—living and working in the developing world. My time in Nepal had been a realization of that desire. Even the VISTA job, domestic though it was, had filled me with a sense of purpose and pride. I'd created something from scratch that would continue after I'd left. I'd had a positive impact on peoples' lives. I'd made a difference.

But that feeling had long since gone. My VISTA position had ended around the time that I got sick and I felt too worn out to make a big move, job-wise. So I made a small one, becoming the agency's volunteer coordinator. I plodded along in my job. I processed applications and attended volunteer recruitment fairs. I planned the agency's first-ever volunteer appreciation party. I missed working directly with the clients. I wasn't fulfilled, but I felt too sick to muster the energy to do anything about it. This was what Crohn's did, I thought. Sapped. Leached the colour out of everything.

And the hurt feeling about Beth and Kevin's departure? That was more complicated. We had other friends, of course, most of them co-workers or friends of college friends who were also recent Seattle transplants. But Beth and Kevin were our first couple friends, our closest friends. Beth, who'd lived in Seattle half her life, served as my unofficial ambassador. She was the one who told me about the best breakfast spots and bookstores. She helped translate the music section of Seattle's independent newspaper, *The Stranger*, each week and decide which bands to go see. Though standing around smoky bars listening to bands I'd never heard of wasn't my favourite pastime, I still did it regularly. We all did, as though going out to hear music was part of our job description.

Ditto for large parties, which I attended whether I felt in the mood to socialize or not, lest I miss out on something. I preferred more intimate gatherings where we each brought food to share or took turns crowding into someone's kitchen to prepare dinner together. Beth and I co-hosted a monthly dinner where everyone spoke only Spanish. She was the principle player in my social life, second only to Matt. I saw her every day at work and most weekends. I couldn't imagine my Seattle life without her.

I shouldn't have worried about losing touch. Like me,

Beth remained close to friends from all parts of her life, surmounting geographical barriers and harried schedules to make time to see them. Matt and I had even talked about going to Ecuador for a visit. But I did worry. Maybe I had a hunch, buried deep and barely detectable. When she moved back to Seattle, if she moved back, things would not be the same between us.

\*\*\*

One evening that spring a few months before the move, I perched at the foot of Beth's bed as she zipped back and forth from bedroom to bathroom, getting dressed to go to a karaoke bar. The outing would be our mutual friend's send-off from urban life; she'd recently married and would be moving to the suburbs. While Beth searched for a scarf to match her blouse, we talked about our friend.

"We won't be seeing much of her anymore," Beth said.

"What do you mean?" I asked.

"That's what happens. People get married, move to the 'burbs. They'll pop out a couple of kids and then forget all about us childless un-marrieds." She would make new friends, Beth said. It was hard to imagine. The friend was a central figure in our group of co-workers that got together on the weekends for dinner parties or outings to the bar. Was she really going to become one of Those People?

"Are you going to get married?" I asked Beth once, early in our friendship.

"Did my grandma tell you to ask me that?" Beth's family was Catholic, and Beth took pleasure in eschewing the traditions of the religion she found distasteful. Beth thought marriage was patriarchal, oppressive. Since gay people couldn't marry, straight people shouldn't either. Marriage was an institution, she said. The only institutions she was interested in being part of were ones that would assign her papers and award her a degree.

Beth always liked a good debate. Probably she wanted me, or someone, to argue with her, to host a Point/Counterpoint episode in her living room. Or else I should sign an oath, pinky-swear that I wouldn't get married. But I was ambivalent. Whenever the topic came up, I'd nod my head noncommittally. We got ready to leave.

"Okay," I said as I patted myself down, making sure I had everything. "Okay. Okay. Okay." I performed this routine regularly, an imitation Peter Falk in his role as a narrating grandfather from *The Princess Bride*. We'd all seen the movie enough times that its dialogue got worked into our conversations, becoming the language of our friendship.

"Stop rhyming now, I mean it!" Beth said from her doorway.

"Anybody want a peanut?" I said as I stepped past her and down the steps. Beth flipped the porch light on and locked the door. She paused at an anaemic-looking bush by the front step, two pink flowers struggling to bloom.

"Come on, Ms Camellia," Beth said, stroking the broad green leaves, her face close to the plant. "You can do it."

We climbed into my car. I took a medication that came with an alcohol contraindication, so I'd become the group's designated driver. I'd never been a big drinker and I was used to cheerfully accompanying my friends on bar outings. On that evening, though, as I circled the blocks surrounding the bar looking for parking, then wedged myself into a chair at the too-crowded table in the too-loud bar, I wondered whether I should have come. Who participates in an evening of karaoke sober?

We ordered (club soda for me, pitchers of margaritas and

tequila shots for everyone else) and then I sat at the table while the members of our group took turns getting up to sing. Beth and our friend preparing to move to the suburbs browsed the binder of karaoke songs.

"The Eagles!" our friend shouted. Beth burst out laughing.

"At any given time," Beth liked to say, "somewhere in the world, an Eagles song is playing."

"We have to do The Eagles," our friend said.

"Clearly," Beth said. "No other choice." So they sang a duet of "Take it to the Limit." With Beth's encouragement, most of the bar joined in on the chorus, and they received the evening's largest round of applause.

On the way home, Beth chattered drunkenly while I navigated the dark streets, fighting to stay awake.

"What's Ecuadorian food like?" I asked. "Will you be expected to overthrow your vegetarianism?" She wrinkled her nose.

"Under no circumstances will I eat *cuy*."

"What is *cuy*?" I asked.

"Guinea pig." She lifted her arms up to her chin and bent her hands down in an imitation. "*Cuy!*" she said in a soft squeal. She went on to describe other food she was more excited about: fresh-squeezed juice, a fried plantain dish called patacones. She told me she planned to eat an entire avocado every day.

"For the whole year?" I asked.

"Yes," she said. "365 avocados. And then I'll come home."

"Don't go," I said, mock-distressed.

"To Ecuador?"

"Yes. What will I do without you?" I forced my voice an octave higher than usual so I'd sound cartoonish and insincere.

Beth laughed. "You'll coordinate some volunteers," she

said. "You'll see some bands." Matt and I had agreed to store some of Beth and Kevin's belongings while they were gone.

"I'll watch your TV and eat all of the canned pumpkin."

"And then you'll come visit," she said.

"And then we'll come visit."

It was well after midnight, and bright lights emanated out toward us from buildings that lined the street: the movie theatre marquee, the twenty-four-hour supermarket's neon rooftop sign, the customer-choked parking lot of the burger stand. I turned off the arterial onto Beth's street and pulled up in front of her house. She unbuckled her seat belt and opened her door.

"Thanks for driving so I could drink," she said. "Lunch Monday?" Unless one of us had a meeting, we ate lunch together every weekday, trading bites like middle-schoolers. She'd introduced me to quinoa, and I'd converted her from mustard-hater to mustard-lover.

"Of course," I said. Beth climbed out of the car and walked up the path. Just as she'd done when we left the house, she paused at the camellia plant and brushed her hand over it. As she stepped up to unlock the door and go inside, one pink petal dislodged itself from the bush and fluttered onto the rain-slicked pavement. I sat in my idling car looking at the doorway that had framed her body just a moment before.

*Lunch Monday?* A phrase from *The Princess Bride* floated into my mind, the one Westley uses to substitute for "I love you" when wooing young Buttercup. The rain and the clack of the windshield wipers and the night swallowed my words as they moved from my brain to my vocal chords and emerged from my mouth.

"As you wish."

# 6. Truco

Beth's laugh announced her presence from the other side of the immigration desk at Quito International. As I scanned the crowd I heard the familiar bubble of sound rising above the din of greeters welcoming passengers. Once Matt and I reached the front of the line, Beth was easy to spot. In Ecuador she stood tall, her long red hair and pale face even more distinctive than at home. It had been eight months since she and Kevin had left Seattle. Beth's eyes found mine, and she started waving like a kindergartner on stage at a school play.

"You're here!" she said when we came across the customs line at last. She wrapped me in a hug, her arms pressing into my shoulders and my overstuffed backpack. We crossed diagonally, Matt and Beth hugging as I hugged Kevin, his smile radiating from beneath his baseball cap.

We headed outside into the humid midnight air and climbed into an awaiting taxi. I watched Matt's eyes take in the chaotic scene with a combination of wonder and fear. Prior to our trip he'd only left the U.S. by car. He felt uncomfortable in unfamiliar surroundings, and didn't like anyone to know his tourist status. When we visited other cities, he would study the map at night in the hotel room so that he didn't have to pull it out on a street corner. His posturing as a local wherever we went seemed to work, as people often asked him for directions. As the taxi wound its way through Quito's dense outskirts to our hotel, I imagined Matt's thought process as he looked out the window. How will I ever find my way around? What happens if Janet gets sick while we're here? I reached over and squeezed his hand.

***

In the morning I transferred my medications from our carry-on bags to our duffel. For night time, cortisone in both liquid-enema and suppository form. In the mornings I swallowed twelve pills that varied in appearance and pronounce-ability: Sulphasalazine, Asacol, Imuran, Mercapto-purine. Chalky, amber, tan, white. Round, oblong, tiny, the length and thickness of a baby's pinky.

In the aftermath of my abscess Dr Frances won a months-long campaign she'd been mounting and convinced me to take steroids. By the time I arrived in Ecuador, a few months after I started the Prednisone, I displayed nearly every side effect listed on the prescription insert. Acne covered my neck, chest, and upper back like a rash. Dark hairs appeared on my chin and in a spiral around my navel. I experienced daily headaches, low libido, irritability. A layer of fat termed "buffalo hump" appeared at the nape of my neck. My metabolism got thrown out of whack; I felt hungrier than ever and began consuming portions worthy of an Olympic athlete in training. I gained twenty pounds, fifteen of which seemed to be on my face, balloons inflated in each cheek and under my chin. *Moon face*, the prescription insert called the swelling. On forty milligrams, my initial dose, my cheeks swelled to the point that my eyes almost disappeared. I looked like Violet Beauregarde in *Charlie and the Chocolate Factory*, inflating into a giant blueberry.

"Do you want to visit a faith healer while you're here?" Beth said as the four of us rode a bus north to the mountain town of Otavalo later that morning. "You'll have to bring him a carton of cigarettes and a can of Sprite," she said. "He uses them as diagnostic tools."

"No thanks."

Beth and Kevin lived atop a steep hill a mile above Otavalo. Kevin worked in a variety of roles: English teacher, environmental educator, construction worker. He built the tiny house where they lived, learning Spanish from the local men as they stood side by side, spreading mortar on cinderblocks.

Beth worked as the administrator for the town's only medical clinic. She took the position to a new level and trained locals to promote the concept of preventive care. She worried that the clinic would cease to function after she left, so she provided mentorship to the locals, hoping they would advocate for themselves in her absence.

It became immediately clear that there, as in Seattle, Beth and Kevin were cherished members of the community, already at the centre of its orbit. They were godparents for two different families, and the un-Ecuadorian name "Kevin" was bestowed upon three babies born during their stay. I envied so much: Beth's language fluency, her obvious comfort in this foreign place, her health. She beamed as she walked around town. I wanted that beam.

In the evenings, we went out to hear music or play cards. Beth and Kevin taught us an Argentinean card game called *Truco*. I observed that it sounded like an epithet, and it became our word for the trip. The bus was late—*truco*! We lost our way on one of Otavalo's back roads—*truco*!

The four of us stayed overnight at a resort in Chachimbiro, soaking in hot springs and playing cards by candlelight during the rainstorm-induced power outages. While the electricity was off, I imagined bacteria gathering on the chicken carcasses lining the refrigerator case at the front of the restaurant. The menu offered one meal for dinner: chicken soup. The next day, it took its revenge on me.

My symptoms were more acute than my regular Crohn's manifestation, and it felt like my energy drained further with each restroom visit. Developing countries each have their own way of managing inadequate plumbing. Ecuadorians throw their toilet paper into a plastic mesh trash can that occupies every bathroom. For days, our hotel room smelt like shit. I worried. Matt worried.

"Any better today?" he said every morning when I woke, sun already pouring through the windows of our all-white hotel room.

"A little," I said. I felt hung-over even though I hadn't had anything alcoholic to drink the entire trip. I tried to be game, staying at the budget hotel instead of the fancy one on the other side of town, travelling to a hot springs by bus and returning when I felt so sick I could barely stand. We were able to afford a more luxurious vacation, a five-star hotel, a hired driver. I could have taken naps in the afternoons instead of sight-seeing. But I felt embarrassed about my illness and ashamed of needing special accommodation. It wasn't like a broken leg or a case of chicken pox. It was messy. It was private. It was shit.

***

Three days after our return from the hot springs, Matt and I rode a taxi up the hill from Otavalo to Beth and Kevin's house. My nausea had abated, but the diarrhea hadn't stopped. It didn't seem to matter what I ate, so when Beth suggested we come to her house to make *llapingachos*, potato pancakes topped with thick dollops of peanut sauce, I agreed.

We arrived to find Beth standing at her stove frying potatoes in a pool of oil. Sunbeams reached through iron-barred windows to splash on the concrete floor. In the middle of the high wooden table, a bunch of bananas rested in a white ceramic bowl painted with orange flowers. I sat on a stool and worked on mustering an appetite. Beth looked across the kitchen at me. She cocked her head to the side, a trademark tilt.

"What's the matter with you?" she said, blunt as ever. I described my symptoms, the ways in which they were different from my usual state of being. She listened and nodded. Here she was on her day off from her role as medical advocate for the community, performing the same role for me.

"Okay," she said when I finished my explanation. "Here's the plan."

The next morning she took me to the doctor who worked at Beth's community clinic. She had an office near our hotel in Otavalo, not a tourist clinic, but as a friend of Beth's I got special treatment. I handed her the letter Dr Frances wrote, translated by my neighbour, a doctor who spoke fluent Spanish. Beth and I sat across the desk from the doctor while she read the letter, like a married couple signing papers at a lawyer's office. I started out responding to her questions in Spanish, with Beth correcting my grammar. I was low on brain capacity, though, and after a few questions, I responded only in English. Beth translated matter-of-factly, relaying the details of stool frequency and colour.

"*Amarillo y café*," she told the doctor, giving me a sideways smile that said both "you knew that one" and "I'm sorry your shit is yellow."

The doctor sent us to the pharmacy to buy a sample cup, and Beth and I wore a triangular path between pharmacy, doctor's office, and analysis lab, me carrying an open container with my own faeces inside. Capturing bodily waste in specimen containers was an action I performed regularly at home, though this was my first time walking my own sample to the lab. The cup, the kind used for urine samples, fit easily in my palm. I clung to the rim of the container, careful not to spill its contents on the street. It was three blocks from the clinic to the lab, and the route was a minefield: tourists, locals, taxis, food carts, souvenir stands, dogs, musicians all competing for space on the narrow dirt road.

It was Saturday, which meant Otavalo's street market was in full swing. Booths lined the town square, fanning out from the centre for several blocks. Tables showcased a riot of colours: serapes, sweaters, jewellery, and tapestries. In one corner, black soapstone and Tagua nut carvings of all shapes and sizes, in another, products from the nearby towns Matt and I had visited with Beth: leather from Cotocachi, weavings from Ambato.

An hour after we dropped the sample off, Beth and I returned to the lab to get the results. We sat in hard plastic chairs in the hall. Through the doorway, we saw the technician sitting at the microscope. She held a mango popsicle as she analyzed a slide, holding it protectively away from the scope as she pressed her eye against the lens.

"Won't the popsicle taint the sample?" Beth whispered to me. We laughed, first under our breaths, and then louder, the laughter echoing in the hallway. The technician snapped her head up at the noise and wrote something on a slip of paper. She folded the paper into an envelope and called out something in Spanish that I didn't understand. Beth got up and walked over to retrieve the envelope from the tech's free hand. We went back to the doctor's office, and she read the results. Her eyes widened in surprise. *Truco.*

"*Amoebas!*" she said. "*Es increíble!*" I felt twin emotions of anger and relief. Everyone else ate the same bacteria soup at the hot springs; my compromised immune system and my defective intestines made me the sole victim. But a specific diagnosis offered more direct options than a vague one. More pills to ingest, yes, but unlike the others I took, these would provide a cure.

One more trip to the pharmacy, where, waiting in line, we speculated as to whether or not the popsicle also had amoebas, and what its treatment might have been. On our way back to my hotel Beth took my elbow and steered me toward a market booth.

"Let's get you something to go with that case of amoebic dysentery," she said. She walked me to a table covered in the ubiquitous bracelets I'd admired since we arrived in Otavalo. Tiny, bright, seed-shaped beads ring the wrists and necks of most of the women there. Beth told me to choose a bracelet, and I selected a cobalt one. She fished some *sucres* out of her purse, and after bargaining a price, wrapped the bracelet around my wrist. I slid it up and down, rolling the beads around with my fingers, an action I would perform every time I wore it. I felt surprised at its beauty, how it dressed up my arm, my diseased and dysenteried body.

"There," Beth said. "Feel better already?"

I did.

# 7. The Goddamn Grand Canyon

In late spring two months after our Ecuador trip, Matt and I went rafting through the Grand Canyon. Every evening the desert heat dissolved into a chilly dusk and the guides built a fire. I liked to sit directly to the side of the blaze, feeling its warmth while the flames stood on the periphery of my view: the steep canyon wall covered in shadow, the sandy bank giving way to the Colorado, indigo in the evening light. I wrote in my journal, or read, or stared into space while the rest of the group bustled around me—the guides preparing dinner, the other guests standing in clusters, beers in hand, talking and laughing.

One of our last days on the river, while I sat fireside in my pre-dinner reverie, Bob dropped his camp chair on the sand next to mine.

"Mind if I join you?" he said.

"Please do."

Bob and his wife Cynthia were among my parents' closest friends, dating back to Dad and Bob's college and medical school days. Bob was the friend who'd suggested I go see the G.I. specialist in Seattle that he knew, the offer I'd refused at the beginning of my Crohn's treatment. Their middle son had organized the raft trip as a celebration of his medical school graduation the following month. My mom, Matt, and I joined the group halfway through, hiking from the canyon's South Rim to Phantom Ranch to take the spots of three people who'd hiked out that morning.

Bob folded his six foot-plus frame into a sitting position. He wore the same horn-rimmed style glasses and thick moustache he'd had since the 1970s. We chatted for a few minutes.

"So," he said finally, and a long pause followed. "How are you feeling? How's your Crohn's?"

What emotions must have stirred within him the first time he saw me coming across the suspension bridge at Phantom Ranch, a person he'd known since birth, a healthy, active girl? I had a flare-up every time I tried to wean myself off the Prednisone, so I was on a small maintenance dose indefinitely. I still had all of the medication's side effects. I weighed 150 pounds, a substantial load to bear for my five-foot-two-inch frame. My wide-brimmed hat accentuated my weight gain and swollen face like a fun-house mirror.

To make matters worse, I'd tripped coming out of the Porta Potty at the top of the trail on the south rim the morning we hiked in, and sprained my ankle. My mom lent me her hiking pole, and I hobbled down seven miles of steep trail, slipping often, worsening the sprain every few steps. No wonder Bob had walked right past me as I limped across the bridge, his eyes scanning the trail behind me for the petite, vibrant young woman of his memory.

The ugliest part of me, though, resided somewhere inside of me. Not my diseased intestine, but the shadowy matter that made up the fibres of my soul. I'd become bitter about my illness, resenting the healthy status of those closest to me.

The person who bore the brunt of this, of course, was Matt. We'd quit our jobs in February and were both sched-

uled to start school the following month, June—Matt for
civil engineering, me for library science. Four months to
travel and play had sounded luxurious when we planned it
the previous fall. Spending every waking moment together,
though, had started to take its toll, at least on me. By the
time the raft trip arrived, I felt tired of Matt's company. Or
rather, I thought I needed a break from my kind, patient
boyfriend instead of understanding the obvious—that it
was life as a Crohn's patient I wished to escape. Having a
chronic illness had started to feel like an endurance race
and I didn't know if I had the stamina for it. Of course, I
could no more part ways with my lifelong, incurable disease than I could have left one of my limbs back in Seattle.

Matt showed no signs of relationship fatigue. On our
hikes into the narrow side canyons he would come up behind me.

"Look Janet," he would say in my ear. "It's the goddamn
Grand Canyon." He was quoting a line from *Thelma and
Louise*. I'd always laugh, but the phrase stuck with me
through the trip. Maybe it was the shit-coloured glasses
through which I viewed life, but I didn't feel a swell of gratitude for getting to see one of the seven natural wonders
of the world and going on a trip many dream of but fewer
actually take. Instead, I felt surprised by how much brown
existed there. On its flat stretches, the Colorado looked less
like the western rivers I'd grown to love and more like a
farm pond full of pesticide-coated mud. The rock varied in
colour, some red and white mixed in with the tan. I tried
to absorb the guides' explanations of the different canyon
layers and types of rock, Kaibab, Supai, Tapeats, Vishnu;
sandstone, limestone, shale, schist.

Something remained more prominent in my mind about
the earth that surrounded us, though: it was too rigid to

dig a hole. I panicked when I learnt that we were only allowed to poop in the portable toilets the raft company provided. They got packed onto their own passenger-less raft every morning, not to be set up again until evening. If we had an emergency we could use the container reserved for such purposes, a plastic tub that once held margarita mix. Stamped diagonally across the front in perky blue script was the message, "tastes great with tequila!" I did not use the emergency toilet. Instead, morning to evening, I clenched. Goddamn Grand Canyon, indeed.

I developed a crush on one of the raft guides, and harboured fantasies of following him to Utah after the trip to go climbing. Matt registered my flirtations internally, he told me later, but said nothing while we were rafting. He was trying, had been trying all these years, to look past my illness, to not let it take a toll on me, on us. But I couldn't ignore it. It felt as though I was in a raft all by myself, trying to negotiate the mansion-sized boulder that had plunked itself down in the middle of the river after the rest of the group had already made it further downstream.

\*\*\*

I'd rafted the Colorado before, on the stretch that ran close to the ski town where I lived after college. I went on a day trip with my friends and our next-door neighbours, three men whom we'd met the day before. The only one of our six-member group who had more than a couple of raft trips under his belt was the boat's owner, Doug. His two housemates, who'd moved from New Jersey to Colorado the previous month, had never been in a raft.

As I stood at the put-in watching the higher-than-average river rush past me, one thought bubbled to the surface: this is a very bad idea. But my extroverted friend wasn't protesting, so I kept my mouth shut. We set off with me in the back, opposite Doug. Soon enough, we heard the rush of water ahead, louder than our voices. We came around the bend and saw a large rock dead-centre of our first rapid.

"Paddle right, hard!" Doug screamed as we headed left, and straight over the top of the rock. We tipped vertically onto the hole the water formed around the rock and the boat stayed in that stuck position, wedged between the hole and the rock as if with Velcro. Doug and I were forced to our feet, and I heard him say "shit" as I launched out over the boat and into the water.

The underside of the rapid was the opposite of its surface. Cold, quiet, and dark, it was like being in a slow, mute washing machine. I knew almost nothing about whitewater rivers, but I did know this: a hole can hold an object a long time, longer than the average human lung capacity. It releases you when it feels like it. The river flowed over, under, all around me. Time slowed almost to a stop as water pushed me backwards into the hole. I thrashed wildly, to no effect. Nearly out of breath, I had no choice but to submit. My limbs went still, and almost immediately, I spat out of the hole. I popped to the surface, my feet pointed, mercifully, downstream. I imagined bouncing off rocks, first with my feet, then with my head. I thought of my helmet still fastened to the raft. Bad, bad. Stupid, stupid, stupid.

But the impact never came. The current slowed. I remembered I could swim and did so, landing in an eddy further downstream. I scrambled onto the bank, a thin swath of dirt abutted by large rocks. Doug and one of my friends had fallen out too—they climbed onto the bank alongside me. Somehow the other three managed to get the boat to the eddy and hold it there. The water flowed by at some forty thousand cubic feet per second, a herd of buffalo charging past. The river had a lesson to teach me that day, but it would take me years to hear it: trust your inner voice and speak up. If you don't, you might die.

***

Sitting with Bob in the middle of the Grand Canyon, I wasn't sure how to answer his simple question—*how are you?* Had he seen my wordless exchanges with the head guide each night as he fished my "refrigerated" medicine out of the water at the bottom of his raft? Did he know about the liquid enemas I squeezed into my rectum each night while lying in the tent I shared with Matt, the used bottles I stored in a Ziploc in my duffle, folded against themselves like empty beer cans? Maybe it was all obvious to Bob: my flirtations, my moving around in my body like it didn't belong to me. He had five children, after all, including two daughters around my age.

The dinner preparations grew louder—a clatter of pots on the four-burner camp stove, the *chopchopchop* of the knife mincing cabbage and carrots—and I saw my opening, a moment where my words would be inaudible to the rest of the group.

"It's been frustrating," I said, finally. And then the rest came tumbling out. I told him about the attempts to manage my symptoms, the long list of medications I'd tried, the bi-weekly visits to the acupuncturist, the tea. I'd started seeing a naturopath, who planned to put me on an elimination diet as soon as I got back from Arizona. It was like a child-constructed rock dam giving way; once I started talking, I couldn't stop. Finally I got to the Prednisone. My gastroenterologist still seemed unconcerned about my side effects; I found them worse than the disease itself.

"I think we've come to an impasse," I said. "She says there are no other medications for me to try." This wasn't totally true; there was one more option, a medication recently approved by the FDA. It was only available intravenously, though. I'd have to go into the clinic for regular infusions, like a chemomapy treatment. No thanks.

"You know about the clinic director," he said, referring to him by a nickname. "Your Dad told you about our connection?"

"Yes," I said. "But won't my doctor be offended if I go somewhere else?"

"It's your right as a patient," he said. "People do it all the time." He asked me if he should give me the phone number.

"I'll look it up," I said.

"How about I call you in a month," he said, "to make sure you've found it." It was a therapist's move, the deadline-setting. I took my first deep breath in months, letting it out in a long exhale. I felt like I'd lost weight since sitting down.

"Sounds good," I said. "Thanks for asking."

"Glad I did," Bob said. Matt joined us on the sand and I scooted my camp chair closer to his. I rested my hand on his knee. Matt pointed to the top of the canyon.

"Look," he said, and Bob and I tilted our heads in the direction of his finger. On the uppermost ledge sat a tiny arch. Through its miniature frame you could see a few inches of sky, and a star framed in its exact centre. How many of those sights had I missed on this trip, busy brooding?

"Good eye," Bob said. I thought he might launch into the long explanations he was prone to, something about the geological history of the canyon. But like Matt and me, he was quiet. Behind us, one of the guides banged on a pot behind us three times in rapid staccato.

"Hot soooup," he yelled, drawn out, like a sheepherder calling his flock home for the night.

# 8. Out of Order

"I don't think you have Crohn's Disease," the doctor said from his position on a stool at one end of the exam room. He was the doctor Bob had recommended, whom I'd called without prompting a few weeks after we returned from the Grand Canyon. My heart ping-ponged across my torso.

"I don't have Crohn's? What do I have?"

"There's something going on outside your intestine. A growth."

"A growth." It was so much to process, like when I'd first been diagnosed two years before. Apparently all I could do was repeat what he said back to him. Reflective listening, they call that in therapy circles. I didn't feel reflective. I was in shock. I thought this doctor would simply have a new course of treatment for me, maybe take me off Prednisone, which I'd been taking for nearly a year. But no Crohn's Disease? That seemed impossible.

"The growth is pushing through to the inside of your rectum," he said. It was causing Crohn's-like symptoms, but it wasn't Crohn's. He rolled his stool over to the exam room desk. He was the same height as my Dad, with the same freckle pattern on his bald head. This doctor, though, had an olive complexion, and wore a button-down-and-sweater combination to see his patients rather than the tie my Dad preferred. He wrote down the name of a surgeon in Seattle who had operated on his wife.

"You should talk to a surgeon at Mass General too," he

said. "The more opinions, the better. I'm sure your Dad knows someone." He hadn't remembered my father from medical school, but he recognized his name, causing him to refer to me as "the Buttenwieser girl," to his nurses when he thought I was out of earshot.

So, Matt and I got on an aeroplane. We must've looked like a normal young couple going on vacation, my short frame tilted against his tall one as the plane ascended and hurtled past Mount Rainier as it stood like a sentry guarding the wilderness. I'd only been to the national park that surrounded the mountain twice before, once with Beth, once with Matt.

"I want to go camping," I said. It was September, the perfect month for northwest camping, the tourists returned home and the weather still sublime. Matt turned away from the window to give me a sympathetic smile. Camping was an impossibility for me right then.

"Next summer we'll do a big trip," he said. "Epic."

In Boston, more scans, more lying on my side to endure the intestinal scope. Part of having a unique set of symptoms meant submitting to the same battery of tests each time I saw a new doctor. Maybe medical establishments were like spy organizations or the mafia in that way, only trusting the intel that came from inside their own group. Or maybe it was just their way of revealing the fact that, despite appearances to the contrary, medicine was not an exact science. What one set of radiologists had determined was an abscess, a new group of doctors was now calling a growth. Removable. Curable.

My parents came with me to the appointment. My mom wore a fuchsia blouse and her trademark purple Converse high tops. My father's thick bifocals, usually smudged with fingerprints, had been cleaned for the occasion. How would

it feel to accompany your twenty-eight-year-old daughter
to the doctor, to look at her and know she had a cyst growing inside her, this person that you created, birthed, and
raised? The three of us sat shoulder-to-shoulder in the doctor's fluorescent-lit office as he made his pronouncement,
the same as the doctor's in Seattle: not Crohn's Disease. A
tumour.

In the space of two months, my lifelong, chronic disease that affects approximately 500,000 Americans became
a temporary problem that seemed fixable. The thought of
shedding my incurable status thrilled me. At the university, I'd been just another person with Crohn's. With this
new diagnosis, I became a once-in-a-career patient. Teams
of distinguished doctors would hold meetings about me.
They'd sit around a glossy table discussing what kind of
growth might be inside of me, and how to get it out. They
would pour their expertise into my case. I felt like a princess. These were my suitors. One of them would cure me.
There would be a happy ending.

But sitting there in the surgeon's office, just a few miles
from Boston Women's Lying-In Hospital where I was born,
it all began to sink in. Abdominal surgery, with its accompanying pain and fatigue. Putting myself completely at the
mercy of the doctors. They were the experts, and I had to
do what I was told without protest, submitting to numer-
ous tests, pokes, and prods. I was not a princess; I was a
case. I felt fortunate to be in the position I was in, receiving
care from some of the best doctors in the country, maybe
the world. But in the end, privilege would only buy me so
much. I was still a patient. I still had to be cut open.

\*\*\*

Back in Seattle, the impossibly clear water in the exotic fish tank was the first sign that I'd stepped up to a higher level of medical care. I sat in the waiting room and filled out paperwork. There were a handful of other patients, all of them middle-aged or elderly, accompanied by their spouses. The nurse greeted each of them by name and brought them back to the exam rooms to wait some more.

After I'd finished my paperwork and watched the black-and-yellow-striped fish make a few laps around the tank, it was my turn to follow the nurse past the reception desk and into an exam room. Three floor-to-ceiling windows revealed a view of downtown, and Elliott Bay beyond. Puffs of clouds drifted lazily by the window, in no hurry to block the August sunlight. My pulse quickened as the door closed behind me. What was the doctor going to tell me? Would he confirm what the other two doctors had said, his affable colleague here in Seattle and the stern surgeon from Boston?

A confident knock on the door, and in strode a six-and-a-half-foot tall man in a long white coat. He introduced himself as Tom. He extended a slender-fingered hand and smiled to reveal a set of straight teeth. His eyes met mine to punctuate the well-polished greeting.

Dr Tom did not sit down. He told me he'd looked at my chart. If he were to perform my surgery, he said, he would do it with another doctor from the same hospital.

"We are the two best colorectal surgeons on the West Coast," he said, beaming. I don't know what authority originally made this pronouncement, but sitting there in the exam room, I was impressed. I felt a surge of flattery: me, worthy of being operated on by a team of stellar surgeons. He opened the door and stepped aside to let me walk through first.

"Let's take a look at your films."

The results of a CT scan I'd had the week before sat in a large envelope tucked under his arm. The film reader was located across the hall. We wound our way across the plush carpet to the other side of the u-shaped hallway.

The reader was not in another room, as I had understood, but actually in the hallway itself. Dr Tom slid the films out of their sleeve and into their slots in one fluid move-ment. He flipped a switch and the reader lit up, exposing my lower half: pelvic bones, coccyx, abdomen, colon. He pointed to a golf-ball-sized white area, near the bottom of my spine. This was the growth that radiologists at the uni-versity hospital had identified as an abscess, the one that required repeated scans and full-throttle antibiotics.

"Here's where your problem is," he said, tapping the film with his index finger. He did not think it was an abscess. He thought it was a growth, probably benign, but one that needed to come out. Perhaps it was his lanky figure evok-ing thoughts of high school athletics, but in the hallway, I began to feel not so much like a patient as a member of a basketball team standing in front of the chalkboard while Coach outlined the plan for Saturday's game. Looking at my own films, it wasn't hard to separate my mind from my body, floating above the conversation as though this were someone else's surgery we were discussing. I smacked back down to earth when he said, "You're probably looking at a permanent colostomy."

"What?" was all I could manage.

"We'd take out your rectum, your anus," he told me. "It's hard to tell for sure where this mass is until we open you up, but it looks too low to me to be able to give you any function in your colon." He went on to explain that, if things were better than he expected, he would just remove my rectum and use part of my upper colon to form a new one. "It's called a j-pouch," he said. He was talking fast, like a car salesman. It was too much information to process. I wanted to leave. But I was rooted to the carpet, my eyes locked on my film, the white mass. I could feel it inside me, like someone's thumb pressing into my tailbone as if it were a piece of clay they were trying to sculpt into a wine goblet or a vase.

A door opened beside us and an older doctor emerged from his office. I hoped that my doctor would take down the films, suggest we continue the conversation back in the privacy of the exam room. Instead, the two men greeted one another, and, ignoring me, they looked up at the ceiling above their heads to the fluorescent lights, one square grey from a burnt-out bulb.

"That light has been out of order for a long time," the older doctor said.

"You're right." They both stood there, heads tilted back, trying to puzzle it out. "Let the girls know," Dr Tom said, gesturing toward the waiting room.

"We are the two best colorectal surgeons on the west coast," he'd said. A hierarchy existed, I understood now, an elitism. "The girls," he'd called the women who ran the office. If they were girls, what was I? I was twenty-eight, hardly a girl, but younger than anyone who worked at the clinic. Too young, perhaps, and too unassertive to think on my feet. To say: *I don't care if you're the best colorectal surgeon in the world. No fucking way are you giving me a colostomy.*

\*\*\*

Time clipped by in the month leading up to my surgery. The middle-aged men conferred about my case: the medical school colleague, Dr Tom, and the second surgeon, Dr Stan. Even my father got involved over the phone, treated as a fellow expert even though he practiced psychiatry. No one seemed sure what the surgeons would find when they opened me up, or whether or not they'd be able to remove it.

If all went well, they'd be able to remove the entire growth without removing my anus. They would cut my ileum, the place where my small and large intestine met. I would have a temporary ileostomy while my colon healed, and then another surgery four months later to hook the whole intestine back together and close the ileostomy. If, however, Dr Tom's hallway prediction was right, I'd wake up with a permanent colostomy. There were worse scenarios: they weren't sure that they'd be able to get the growth out at all, and, while they all thought it was benign, it could turn out to be malignant.

All this uncertainty added to my pre-surgery anxiety. But there was an exhilarating quality to those weeks too. There was an end to the suffering. I'd awaken from surgery cured. It seemed unbelievable. It was the chronic illness sufferer's dream come true. It seemed unbelievable. I didn't have Crohn's. *I didn't have Crohn's.*

What I did have was insurance. Good insurance. As a full-time student in the library science program, I had enrolled in the university's generous student plan. The low-cost insurance covered eighty percent of expenses until a certain cap, at which point it covered one hundred percent. I would reach the cap in the first hour of surgery.

But a problem arose. Because the coverage started with the fall quarter, the university had a rule that a student needed to be enrolled in at least one class in order to be eligible for the insurance. My surgery was scheduled for

October, less than a month into the quarter. I wouldn't be able to attend class for several weeks following the surgery, maybe even months. How could I enrol in school if I couldn't go?

"It's ironic, isn't it?" the woman at the student finance office said.

I was grateful for the insurance, though it pissed me off to have to jump through hoops to get it. My family could have paid out-of-pocket for the whole thing, if necessary. I'd like to say that I felt lucky to be able to afford the surgery, that I appreciated how fortunate I was to be able to see top-in-their-field specialists. According to census data, I later learnt, 38.4 million Americans had no health insurance the year I had my surgery. If I'd been in a different financial position, I probably wouldn't have been able to get that second opinion. The growth would have gotten bigger, perhaps eventually warranting emergency surgery.

Back then, though, I wasn't thinking about the bullshit that is our country's health care system. I was focused inward: my body, my operation, my miracle cure. I woke each day with a purpose: attend pre-op appointment. Buy a stack of trashy magazines. Book a hotel room for my parents, who were coming to Seattle for the surgery and recovery effort. The daylight faded noticeably earlier each afternoon while I drove around town, the light slanting between tree branches as the leaves changed into their fall attire of yellow, orange, red. I was unaware of the way in which time was about to slow down for me. Soon I'd be watching the season unfurl from my position on the couch, too weak and tired to go anywhere.

The woman from student financial services suggested that I sign up for an independent study. I connected with a librarian I'd done volunteer work for the previous year,

GUTS

and made a plan to assist her in creating curriculum guides to accompany library kits for preschoolers. I would do research on child development and write a paper.

I went downtown to meet with the librarian. I sat in a hard plastic chair in her cramped office while she piled picture books and documents into a cardboard box. The sun, bright behind the opaque window at my back, glinted off the shiny covers of *Bats at the Beach and Lemonade Sun*. After my surgery, I would only be allowed to carry objects that were less than ten pounds. It was strange to think that, in a few weeks, I'd be unable to lift the box she was filling. Her supervisor came into the office to ask her a question, and introduced himself to me.

"Good luck with your knee surgery," he said as he turned to leave. He'd been misinformed, I supposed, or else made an assumption—what other kind of surgery do people my age have?

"It's not knee surgery," I said, "It's intestinal surgery." My smile went a little too wide as I over-emphasized *intestinal*.

"Oh," he said, as his own smile collapsed.

Beth and Kevin had returned to Seattle a few months before, staying with us until they rented an apartment a few miles from ours. Beth enrolled in the public health program at the same university where I attended library school, and began classes a few weeks before my surgery. Kevin got a job renovating a house ten blocks from our apartment. He was recovering from malaria he'd contracted in Ecuador, his energy waxing and waning as the doctor adjusted his medication. I had a similar experience as my body withdrew from the Prednisone I'd had to stop taking the day my surgery got scheduled.

Despite all of their preoccupations, Beth and Kevin were

at our apartment constantly in the weeks before my surgery. Most of our friends had extended vague offers of "let me know what I can do to help." But Beth didn't ask, she just knew. Before the surgery, she'd come with stories from her new classes to distract me. She'd already made her post-operative food delivery plans. She would be part Florence Nightingale, part Nurse Ratched, I could already tell.

The day before my surgery Beth and Kevin came by my apartment to wish me luck. Beth brought gifts: a blue velour frog and a one-inch tall Buddha statue I'd given her for her birthday the previous year.

"Frogs are good luck animals," she said. "And I thought the Buddha could keep you company while you recover."

"So thoughtful," I said, meaning it. "Thank you."

***

The following afternoon I sat in bed in the curtained-off pre-op room, trying to cry quietly so that the other patients wouldn't hear me. Matt and my parents, who'd flown out to Seattle for my surgery, tried to comfort me. I wore a hospital gown and compression stockings to help prevent blood clots. My IV port was in my arm, but the IV itself had not been hooked up yet. I'd already used the toilet for the last time that week. A catheter would get attached to my urethra after they'd administered the anaesthesia. An internal alarm bell sounded inside my head, a wail that increased in volume as the minutes ticked by: You're. About. To have. Surgery!

I remained dry-eyed until the nurse told me that I'd be in a double room even though I'd requested a private one when I filled out the pre-operative paperwork. I couldn't imagine sharing space with a stranger after a major surgery. Would I have to muster the energy to make small talk? Would my roommate watch the ostomy instructional video along with me? I waited until the nurse left to begin crying, but now I couldn't stop.

Dr Stan poked his head through the curtain, and, seeing my tears, gave me a sympathetic smile. He was in his late fifties, slightly plump with a salt-and-pepper beard. He seemed like someone my parents would be friends with; I could picture a younger version of myself discussing my college literature classes with him when he came over for dinner.

"We're going to take good care of you, Janet," he said. "Get you all fixed up."

My father told him of the rooming situation, and Dr Stan nodded. I wasn't his first patient to cry about sharing a room.

"Let me see what I can do," he said, and ducked back behind the curtain. He returned a few minutes later. "I switched you with one of my patients who's having surgery after you. He won't mind. Besides, your Dad's a VIP." I felt a brief beat of guilt, followed immediately by relief. Then the nurse returned.

Time to go upstairs.

In the operating room, the instant the sedative entered my IV, I felt a wave of calm wash over me. Everything would be fine. They would fix me right up. The space didn't match the vision I'd formed from years of watching medical dramas. It was small and very cold. Bowls of surgical instruments lined the shelves on one wall. Only the lights were as they appeared on TV: round, stainless steel fixtures ringed with bright, circular bulbs hung from the ceiling and a few wheeled stands at the edges of the room. Two nurses helped me onto the table. Bob Dylan played softly in the background.

Stan bustled around the room, along with a resident and the anaesthesiologist.

"This reminds me of college," I said. I meant that the combination of the sedative and the lyrics to "Don't Think Twice, It's Alright" coming from a portable stereo I couldn't see reminded me of getting high on tapestried couches, in over-warm dorm rooms. But that was way too much information to form into words.

"Where did you go to college?" the surgeon asked.

"Colorado," I said.

"Beautiful mountains there," he said. I wanted to agree, to talk about mountains I'd hiked in Colorado, the ones I hoped to climb in Washington once I'd recovered. I wanted to tell him that maybe now I'd get a second chance at young adulthood. Maybe I'd be able to do things in their proper sequence and save the sick bed for old age. But in my near-unconscious state I couldn't connect thoughts to words, I could only smile. Someone placed a mask over my face. I coughed.

The harmonica cut out. Dylan called me babe, his voice a whisper. Guitar notes faded as he retreated down the dark side of the road.

# 9. Chief Complaint

When the ambulance came for me the day before Halloween, its interior was lined with paper skeletons. They dangled above me like a macabre army, keeping watch as I lay on the gurney. Thick black straps formed an X extending out from each corner of the stretcher, tethering it to the ambulance hull. Thinner straps pinned me to the mattress, one across my legs, the other across my chest. I rested my hands against my hips, nervously plucking at my baggy cotton sweatpants. I wore thick tan socks with blue bears printed on them, and no shoes. Strands of unwashed hair lay across my face, and I brushed them away carefully, minimizing movement. Matt sat next to one paramedic in the front seat. The other paramedic sat at my right shoulder, a full array of medical instruments and equipment within arm's length.

I was the centrepiece of our tableau, and in the centre of me was the reason we were all here: a gaping hole in my abdomen where my surgical wound had opened. I had not seen the hole, and though I pictured it as small, I felt no reassurance from this fact. I imagined the worst-case scenario: a trip back to the operating table that held my body just two weeks before.

But we weren't talking about the hole. We were talking about traffic. The freeway was unusually jammed for a Saturday morning, and it would be an agonizing crawl to get to the hospital where I'd had surgery.

Matt asked if they could turn on the siren.

"We're only allowed to do that in life-or-death scenarios," the driver replied. Which mine, apparently, was not. It was up to me, the paramedic in the back said, but he would recommend that we go to the university hospital, since it was closest to our house. For a moment, we were just four people in a car, discussing this as though debating which restaurant to dine at. It's your birthday, Janet. You decide.

Through the ambulance's high windows, I caught glimpses of maple branches, red leaves fluttering against a pale blue background. I imagined the people in the cars around us going to soccer games, or to buy Halloween costumes. Maybe they were heading out of town to go hiking, apple picking. I pictured all of these people talking, laughing, adjusting their car radios, while oblivious to the ambulance beside them, the pain and suffering within. I had to decide where to go. I closed my eyes.

"University."

Dr Tom had been proud of the successful surgery, and we all felt relieved by the pathology report sent earlier that week: the tumour was benign.

"It's called a rectal teratoma," Dr Tom said of my growth the day before my ambulance ride. He removed my staples as he spoke, all forty of them plinking into a metal bowl while he talked. "It was like a piece of cement in there," he said. I envisioned him with a small jackhammer, chipping the tumour away. I winced.

Teratomas are growths that develop in utero, he explained. They sit on top of an organ, containing tissue not normally found there. Ovarian teratomas are fairly common; rectal teratomas are rare. For reasons that remained a mystery to my doctors, mine became inflamed and swelled against my intestinal wall. The mucous, blood, pain, frequent bowel movements, were all due to the teratoma's exterior pressure. The abscess hadn't been an abscess at all. It was the teratoma. Now it was gone, removed before it could change from benign to malignant.

"We're presenting your case at a conference and writing a journal article," he said. He beamed. I understood his happiness. I was a once-in-a-career patient. *Thank you for referring this interesting patient to us* the medical form said. My unusual case seemed to have benefitted me. Years later, I wondered if the doctors would have been so attentive had my illness been more run-of-the-mill.

Dr Tom finished removing the staples, and the nurse came over to help me sit up. She pointed to the place halfway down my eight-inch incision, just below my navel. A week before two pin-sized holes had appeared, occasionally oozing drops of clear fluid.

"We see this all the time," the nurse said, taping a piece of gauze over the area. "They'll heal up on their own."

The holes, it turned out, had different ambitions. Getting up from the couch the following morning, I performed the steps they taught me at the hospital: roll to my side, push up to a sitting position. I stood slowly, and midway up, I felt a sharp tug on my belly, as though I were a marionette whose string had been pulled the wrong direction. I sat back down, and called Matt in from the kitchen. He lifted my shirt and peeked under the gauze.

"Okay," he said slowly. "Your wound has opened up a little. Stay right there." He backed into the other room, out of earshot, and called 911.

"Yup," the paramedic said after he arrived and looked under the gauze. "We need to take you to the hospital." Everyone colluded to keep me calm. I did not look at the hole until a week later, with the aid of a mirror. It was far worse than I'd pictured, a valley in the middle of my belly. The curled flesh on either side of the hole faced skyward, as though someone were trying to turn my abdomen inside out.

In the ambulance, the paramedic spoke into the two-way radio. "Twenty-eight year-old female patient complains of dehiscence." He'd taught me this word only moments earlier, the term for a wound opening up. He gave the dispatch nurse my vitals, and signed off.

"Why did you have to say that?" I asked after he hung up, like we were lovers having a quarrel. "I'm not *complaining*. It's a fact." I applied the same energy to being a patient I'd given to being a student or having a job. I did everything the doctors told me to. I cracked jokes with the nurses. I took my medicine, performed my exercises. I was perfect. The paramedic laughed.

"It's just the term we use. It even says it on the form the doctors fill out. *Chief complaint.*"

All these years later, I still prickle when I recall the paramedic's words. Actually, it's stronger than a prickling. I feel angry at the way we patients are portrayed by the medical establishment as whiny toddlers who need a nap. Patient complains of gunshot wound to the head. Patient complains of missing limb following leg amputation. Patient would complain of lung collapse, if patient could breathe.

When we arrive at the emergency room or the doctor's office, we are not defendants appearing before a judge, whose symptoms are alleged until they can be proven by the doctor beyond a reasonable doubt. We are broken, and we need to tell someone about it so he or she can fix us. We aren't complaining. We are informing. And after all, we, not the doctors, are the experts on our own bodies. They may know how to heal us, but only after we explain to them what's the matter. Maybe that should be the terminology: Patient explains. Patient informs. Wise and talented patient enlightens.

But maybe I have it all wrong. Maybe the actual problem was that I didn't complain enough. A misdiagnosis. Countless, unnecessary drugs and medical procedures. Hours and hours of time spent in doctors' offices, waiting rooms, procedure rooms. And then my wound tore open. I should have complained, loudly and often. But I was silent, stoic. I communicated my feelings to my family and friends, but brought few of these emotions to my doctors' attentions. If it weren't for our family friend Bob urging me to get a second opinion, who knows where I would be? Probably still sitting in the clinic, being treated for a disease I did not have.

After wheeling my gurney into the ER admitting area, the paramedics handed me off to the triage nurse.

"Patient is conscious and alert," my backseat paramedic said, smiling at me as he handed the nurse his clipboard. She signed the papers and handed the clipboard back before wheeling me into an exam room. I would not have to go back into surgery, the doctor informed Matt and me, to our great relief.

Matt left the room to call Beth and Kevin, who would give us a ride home from the hospital. When he returned the nurse explained how we would pack the opening with gauze daily until the tissue knitted itself back together. When I asked the nurse why she thought this happened, her response was simple.

"Prednisone."

The effects of the Prednisone still lingered, even though I'd taken my last dose over a month before the surgery. Prednisone's main purpose is to suppress inflammation, clearing the lungs of people in respiratory distress, or, in my case, relieving the pressure of the growth on my intestine. But inflammation is the body's natural response to healing. With the Prednisone still in my system, my abdomen couldn't join itself back together. Thus, the tear. Perhaps they needed to amend the prescription insert of possible side effects: *Weight gain. Acne. Moon face. Flesh-ripping.*

"We hate Prednisone," Matt said to the nurse. That was all the complaining I had the energy for, given voice by my boyfriend. I needed only the smallest validation from the nurse. She nodded at Matt, and then turned to look at me. She gave me a small smile.

"I hate it too."

# 10. Proposal, Revisited

The pathologist who analyzed my tumour in the lab measured it at approximately four centimetres in diameter. It weighed close to nothing. After surgery, though, it felt like a much heavier object had been removed from my body, something closer in weight to the mini-fridge I had in my college dorm room. As my energy increased and I got used to my ileostomy, I began to abandon my position on our couch with increasing frequency. Matt drove me around the city to my favourite café for sandwiches, to the park where we'd take slow walks.

Late autumn eroded the daylight and hammered rain clouds into place above Puget Sound. Inside my body, though, spring had just arrived. My internal stitches dissolved and the skin around my tear grew back together. It felt as though someone had removed the sheet from the canary cage I'd been unknowingly dwelling inside. I spent a measurable part of each day awash in gratitude when I remembered, over and over, that the problem had been a tumour, not an incurable disease. A benign growth, and it no longer lived inside me.

I noticed, for the first time in over a year, how well Matt cared for me. The Crohn's diagnosis had felt like a life sentence to him too, and now we'd gotten our get-out-of-jail-free card. In the glow of those first post-operative months, I had difficulty remembering why I'd had doubts about marriage, why I'd wanted to wait.

\*\*\*

I remembered the words of my eighth grade history teacher, Mr Conway. History class took place right after lunch, which meant that Mr Conway had the unenviable task of prodding a classroom full of thirteen-year-olds out of a post-lunch stupor to teach us about the civil war. One afternoon we arrived to find the day's topic already outlined on the black board and Mr Conway sitting at the head of the table, a navel orange in front of him. We sat down and he gestured to the fruit, resting next to his legal pad, file folder of notes, and silver Cross pen like a still life we were supposed to paint.

"The orange goes to the first person to correctly name my best friend," he said, beaming under his trimmed moustache as he made eye contact with each of us. He wore a green tie and a grey sweater vest, one pocket protector short of the full nerd outfit.

"Greg," one boy said. "Peter," said another. Everyone called out names, famous, common, names it seemed like they'd made up on the spot.

"Nope," said Mr Conway. "Not that either. Keep trying." A smirk remained on his face as the guessing got louder and more frenetic. No one cared about the orange, we just wanted to get the answer right.

My own best friend sat next to me, guessing along with everyone else. My class of forty-five students had been together since pre-kindergarten, ten years by the time eighth grade, the school's penultimate year, arrived. I seemed to change best friends every about every two years, one friend fading into the background of occasional get-togethers as another assumed the role of weekly sleepover companion, gym class partner, nightly phone call recipient.

Mr Conway was a religious man whose conservative views stood in contrast to our hippie parents. He wasn't preachy about this fact, but he did like to sneak in morality lessons wherever he could. I sensed that this might be such an occasion, and suddenly I knew the answer. I raised my hand.

"Kate," I said, his wife's name. He gave the full-toothed version of his smile, pleased with me and with himself for concocting a clever way to impart a life lesson that I'd remember twenty years later: your spouse is your best friend. Not your fishing buddy or your maid of honour or your college roommate. Your husband. Your wife.

"Right you are, Janet," he said, and amid the chorus of groans that followed, reached across the table to hand me the orange.

\*\*\*

I'd like to describe The Proposal, Matt and me on a mountaintop or a sugar-sand beach, the sun setting over the water as Matt knelt at my feet, a ring in his clenched fist. Tears, an embrace. But that's not how it happened. In fact, neither of us remembers the conversation.

We went to the beach often that fall. Maybe it was there that we had our talk. I can picture it: Matt and I moving slowly, holding hands. Clumps of black seaweed and pieces of washed-up garbage creating a high-water line to our right. On the dry sand above, broken bottles and charred wood fragments, the remnants of summer bonfires. The sunset over the water, with the view of the mountain range at the horizon blocked by a bank of clouds. The air fishy, the gulls arguing with the crows, rap music pulsing from a stereo as a car drove by. I stopped walking, and turned to Matt.

"Let's get married." I said. Not a question. An answer.

# 11. Rules of Engagement

At first, Matt and I kept our marriage plans to ourselves. It felt fun to have a secret for the two of us to share, like a pregnancy in its first trimester. Though I enjoyed fantasizing about wedding dates and locations while I lay on our couch, I did not have the energy to plan in earnest.

My ileostomy closure surgery took place on Valentine's Day of 2000. In the pre-op area the anaesthesiologist struggled to find a good vein in my arm. Dr Tom appeared at his shoulder and peered down at the crook of my elbow.

"I have a 6:00 dinner reservation," he said to the anaesthesiologist in a teasing voice.

"You want to put the line in yourself?"

My parents, in town once again for my surgery and recovery, were the first recipients of Matt's and my engagement news on my last night in the hospital. We told them over dinner—sandwiches from Whole Foods—and they rose from their chairs to hug us. A few minutes later my mom stood up again.

"Yay, yay, yay," she said, jumping up and down. I'd never seen my mom jump. She seemed ecstatic. After my discharge, we called Matt's parents and our siblings. Then it was time to begin telling our friends.

A few days after I got home Beth and Kevin came over for a visit. My mom brought us tea, then returned to the kitchen to do dishes while Beth and Kevin took seats opposite Matt and me in our living room. I didn't expect to be nervous. I could say anything to Beth and Kevin. Couldn't I? I cleared my throat. No one looked at me. Matt made a joke and Beth laughed, dipping her head down, her hair falling in front of her face before she tucked it behind her ears, both sides at the same time.

"We have some news," I said, interrupting. My mouth felt dry. The tea was still too hot to drink, but I took a big sip anyway, burning my tongue, and then sloshing liquid over the side of my mug as I set it down. Matt reached over and mopped it up with a napkin. This wasn't how this was supposed to go. I took a breath, and tried again.

"We're getting married."

Beth looked up from her plate.

"What?" The word came out with force. Maybe she'd heard me wrong, that instead of, "We're getting married," she thought I said, "We've decided to breed children and eat them."

"Wow," Kevin said, more gently. "Really?"

Beth sputtered half-sentences.

"How … ? Where … ? When did you decide this?"

I started talking quickly, and Matt chimed in, explaining our recent decision, the far-off, unknown wedding date. I hoped the expression on Beth's face would change, but her brow remained frozen in a furrow of confusion. Of betrayal.

\*\*\*

Other people's opinions don't matter, I tried to assure myself all the time. But it wasn't true. I cared a great deal about what my friends and family thought about my actions. On some level I couldn't access at the moment, Beth's reaction felt unsurprising. I knew she'd feel like I'd lied to her when I supported her anti-marriage views. But it hadn't been a lie. I still believed that gay folks should be able to marry, that the tradition of marriage had too many oppressive elements.

But wasn't there another side to the argument? Maybe one way to make marriage less patriarchal was actually to get married. The more non-traditional marriages, the better. Right? But I didn't voice any of this to Beth. Instead I harboured a secret shame that I wasn't as strong as her, that I remained unwilling to make personal sacrifices to live my values.

\*\*\*

In our apartment, heat seeped out of our teacups. Beth's response to our news—What?—hung in the silence, like a reddened cheek in the moments after a slap. Why aren't you happy for me, I thought to myself. Or, if you aren't happy, couldn't you at least fake it?

"Oh come on," Kevin chided Beth from our living room floor. He turned to us. "Congratulations."

My eyes strayed across the room, resting on a picture from our trip to Ecuador. The day after the doctor from Beth's clinic diagnosed me with amoebic dysentery, Matt and I boarded a boat to tour the Galapagos Islands. In the photograph, a pair of Sally Lightfoot crabs sat in an inch of water, their neon-orange shells glossy against the near-black rock underneath.

I tried to describe the islands to Beth in a letter after we returned home, the surreal, fantastical land teeming with wildlife not found anywhere else in the world. Blue-footed boobies crowded together on scat-splattered rocks by the water's edge, frigate birds stood at cliff edges, inflating the red sacs under their chins in courtship. We watched fifty lizards storm a beach on one island, crawling over one another to find the perfect sleeping rock. The animals, unafraid of people, carried on their feeding and mating rituals while we stood a few feet away, gawking behind our telephoto lenses before climbing back onto the yacht to motor to the next island. In my letter, I likened it to being high for a week. It seemed like a place out of a child's dream world.

"To Fantasy Island," I said, gesturing towards the photograph with my teacup. Matt, Beth, and Kevin turned to look first at me, then at the pair of crabs sitting in the water, mated for life and unafraid.

\*\*\*

Time passed. I recovered from my surgery. We bought our first house, ten blocks from our apartment, and hired our first set of movers. The night before the moving truck arrived, Beth and Kevin helped us shuttle our plants and a couple of lamps from old home to new. The four of us cracked open beers and took turns posing for pictures in the empty living room, our arms spread-eagled to indicate vastness. Beth smiled at me genuinely, no trace of the knife wound I'd left with our engagement announcement.

Matt and I set a wedding date for July of the following year, giving us (mainly me) eighteen months to plan. During that time I finished school and got my first librarian job. Beth continued in her public health program and got an internship at a local foundation that was just opening a global health division. I'd envisioned us meeting on campus for lunch regularly. But we only managed to do so once in the two years we overlapped in school.

Our friend group from work had fractured as more people married, had children, moved to the suburbs or out of the area altogether. I had my group of friends from school and Beth had hers. My program felt like a rubber stamp I needed to be an official librarian, the classes practical but dull. Beth's program, on the other hand, consumed her. She drank in the information, stimulated by her course work, attending lectures in the evenings. When I did see her in those days her cheeks were often flushed, her eyes even more sparkly than usual, as though she'd spent the day doing something physically active outdoors rather than sitting in a classroom.

My engagement announcement seemed to have caused a fissure in our friendship. Our drift apart was gradual, as though we were sister planets that got knocked out of alignment. Beth no longer called to talk through a problem. We got together less often, and when we did our conversations felt more superficial.

The wedding day arrived in late July, sixty degrees and a storm cloud-filled sky. We held the ceremony in an outdoor garden, retreating to the reception hall for dinner and Irish folk dancing before the rain began. My parents had held a party for us in Boston the month before for my extended family and their large collection of friends. The wedding guests mostly consisted of friends from all parts of our lives. We rented a van for our college friends, all staying together in one house, and they moved from wedding event to event as a festive throng.

Friends, in fact, felt like the wedding's theme. One friend made our wedding cake, another played the flute as I walked down the aisle. A college friend registered online to be a minister for the Universal Life Church so that he could perform our ceremony. Another sang "Sweet Thing" by Van Morrison during the ceremony. My college friend Amy arrived a few days early and I handed over my clipboard so that she could take on the role of point person for the day.

I hadn't seen Beth in several months, and in the receiving line, the distance between us felt palpable. She gave me a tepid hug.

"You look lovely," she said in a bad British accent. She was making fun of me on my wedding day. She was mad at me. I felt sure of these things.

A few months after our wedding, I received an email. *Save the date for Beth and Kevin's wedding celebration.* I felt the way Beth must have felt when Matt and I told her about our wedding plans, like I'd been slapped in the face. She'd changed her opinion about marriage, no doubt with the deliberations she brought to every big decision. I heard nothing, though, of her internal struggle. I was not called upon for advice, or to be a listening ear. Though she only lived a few miles away, I found that I missed her. Did she miss me too?

***

The glass-walled reception hall, perched on a hillside, allowed for a clear view of the Olympic Mountains across the bay. I stood at the window, looking out as other guests filtered in behind me, stopping at the bar before approaching the window themselves.

"Beautiful place you live in," a woman said beside Matt and me. Beth's aunt from Minnesota. I turned, and saw Beth out of the corner of my eye. She stood on the dance floor, posing for a photograph. She wore a silk, sleeveless dress, and the burgundy scarf draped over her forearms matched the beads around her neck. She'd worn the same outfit, she told me, at their family-only wedding ceremony in Kevin's hometown of Sitka the previous month.

"Beautiful bride," I said back. Beth turned, revealing her hair spiralled in a bun at the rear-centre of her head. Across the hall our former work friend who now lived in the suburbs came through the broad entryway with her husband and daughter. At the wedding shower the previous month I'd stood with her and Beth in the kitchen and dipped baby carrots into hummus as we talked.

"I'm pregnant!" our friend said. Beth gasped.

"Holy shit!" Beth said, wrapping her in a hug. "Congratulations!" I mimicked Beth's motions, and forced a smile. I'd been trying, and failing, to get pregnant for several months, a fact I discussed only with Matt.

Why did Beth act happy about our friend's baby? Why couldn't she have had the same response when I told her I was getting married? At the time, I didn't see that with me, she was being genuine. She wasn't actually happy for our friend. The excitement was fake. She, too, forced a smile. Maybe she wanted to have children after all, but feared she'd be like her mom, and die when they were young. Maybe she wanted the happily ever after. But she knew something the rest of us failed to see: it doesn't exist.

Once a crowd amassed at the reception, we lined up at the buffet, and then sat at long tables to eat. Beth and Kevin moved from group to group, pausing briefly to chat with each person before moving on. They approached our table.

"Almost time for the dancing?" I asked Beth, gesturing towards the DJ. She gave me one of her trademark looks: half-surprised, half-sceptical.

"You're going to dance?" she said. I was famous among my friends for being anti-dancing.

"I don't dance," I would say when someone suggested going out to a club. "I can't dance."

"It's your *wedding*," I said to Beth. "Of course I'm going to dance." A beat passed as we looked at each other. It would be the last conversation we had for eight months. Up close, I noticed something unfamiliar in her expression. Not just happiness. She glowed.

"Wow," she said. "I'm honoured." Her dress shone ivory against the backdrop through the picture window, the mountains purpled by the setting sun. I wanted to say something to keep her by my side a moment longer, but she'd already turned to move on to the next table. So I spoke to her retreating figure instead.

"The honour is all mine."

# 12. Grand Mal

For a solid thirty minutes, she did not know her own husband. When the paramedics arrived, they asked Beth his name, and she could not tell them. The President of the United States, according to her, was XV21.

"And I did not vote for that son-of-a-bitch," she might have said. Only she didn't. She wasn't in her right mind.

Kevin awoke to the bed shaking, he told me later. It was 3:00 in the morning. An earthquake, he thought, as he came into consciousness. A slight turn of his head was all he needed to realize that the earthquake was only happening to Beth, her limbs flailing, every body part tense and jerking. He made sure she wasn't going to fall off the bed before calling 911. The minutes ticked by as hours, Beth's body in spasms, the sheets tangled around one leg like a jungle vine. Kevin stood by the side of the bed, arms outstretched, willing her synapses to settle themselves. Finally, she stilled. Soon after the sirens sounded, the trucks pulled up, and two paramedics and four fire-fighters crowded into the small attic bedroom. As they gathered around the bed and began asking questions, Beth drew the blankets up to her neck, her eyes wide with confusion and fright.

"You had a seizure," they told her, but she didn't know what they meant. The paramedics could not fit their stretcher up the narrow stairs. They could barely fit themselves up, young, strapping, and outfitted to manage whatever kind of emergency they might encounter. They carried her down to the ambulance in one of her blue Ikea dining room chairs.

***

The volume in the emergency department was loud with other traumas, the waiting room full of drunks and psychiatric patients off their medication. In a back room, Beth's IV fed anti-seizure drugs into her arm, returning her cognitive abilities. She now understood what had happened, and fear overwhelmed her confusion. She'd been sleeping peacefully, and now she was starring in a medical drama. The trauma hospital covered a five-state region, and Beth was the biggest emergency of the night.

The technician brought Kevin into the monitoring room to watch Beth's insides on the screen while she rolled into the scanner tube, alone. Images appeared on the monitor, and the cause of the seizure came into sharp focus: a growth, bright white and the size of a Wiffle ball, on the screen. On her brain.

Kevin told me he saw the tumour and immediately thought of Beth's mom and her death from brain cancer when Beth was sixteen. The radiologist was summoned to deliver the news to Beth. You have a mass, he may have said. Further testing is required. Family began to arrive, and then a few friends. Kevin did not call me from the hospital. My call came later, from a mutual friend dispatched to relate the story he was tired of telling. Beth's insurance card made its way around the hospital, her status as a grants officer for a local foundation revealed.

"Beth tells rich people which global health crises they need to fix," we would say when explaining her job as a grants officer for a local foundation. Now she was a patient in a research hospital whose grant application may have landed on her desk that very month. A nurse came to wheel her from a common area partitioned by striped curtains to a private room with wooden furniture and soothing peach walls. Beth might have inhaled cleanser fumes from the just-mopped corridor while she awaited an MRI and a diagnosis. She tried to sleep, but the noise of nearby patients and the constant interruptions of nurses checking vitals made it impossible. Doctors and interns filed in see her, the young ones interested in the latest medical curiosity. Two neurosurgeons made funding requests of her while she lay in her adjustable bed.

Thirty-six hours after Beth arrived, she was allowed to go home. No definitive diagnosis. The words *tumour* and *cancer*, not uttered aloud, surely loomed in everyone's thoughts. What is it like to walk out of the hospital and get into your car, to use your brain when you have just found out something is growing on it? I never asked her, and she never said.

I wonder what might have happened to Beth and me, if not for the seizure or the cancer. Did we need such a strong jolt to return to one another? Maybe we would never have spoken again. Maybe, in absence of a trauma, we would not have realized how much we stood to lose.

"Beth had a seizure," my friend said on the phone. I sat in my living room, in an identical twin chair to one Beth owned. Rain dripped from bare dogwood branches outside my window. I wanted to run out the door, drive across town and sit beside Beth in her living room and reassure her that everything would be fine. But I believed she was angry with me. Who was I to show up after an eight-month absence, to say what would and would not be okay? Instead I picked up my pen.

*I'm sorry I've been absent. I am here now. How can I help?*

# 13. Driving Miss Peterman

"Can you give Beth a ride home from work tomorrow?" Kevin said on the phone. He called a few days after I mailed the letter to Beth. She'd have surgery soon, he told me, to remove the mass on her brain. She wasn't allowed to drive, because of the seizure. Could I help?

"Of course," I said. "Anything." After we figured out the logistics, Beth wanted to get on the line.

"I'll bet you have a lot of advice to give me right now." Her first words to me in eight months. Her voice was softer than usual, and had lost its confident tone. She sounded scared.

"Pack your thickest socks," I said. We talked for a few minutes about what else she would need at the hospital. I told her I would pick her up at work the next day.

When she got in the car the following afternoon, I felt there was something I was supposed to say, words that would fill the canyon of silence we'd had for most of the previous year.

"Hi," I said, my voice too high and too loud. Then again, more grounded. "Hi."

"Hi." Beth buckled her seat belt, settled a tray on her lap, the kind people use for eating in bed.

"Nice tray," I said as I started the car. Bluegrass music came out of the stereo. Beth didn't like bluegrass. I turned it off.

"Isn't it? My friend Katherine gave it to me." I didn't know Katherine, or any of her friends from work. She went on to tell me how Katherine had gotten her books about brain surgery out of the library. Katherine was making a schedule for friends to sign up to bring meals to the house. Katherine was doing all of the things I would have been doing if I'd been around lately.

"What a nice friend," I said.

"Everyone should have someone like that in their lives," Beth said. She began giving me directions. She and Kevin had bought their first house a few months before, and I didn't know the way there. They lived in West Seattle, a neighbourhood set on a peninsula across the Duwamish River from downtown. Though technically part of Seattle, it felt like a small town unto itself. Traffic gummed-up the peninsula bridge with regularity, slowing the five-mile passage to the city's epicentre. From Matt's and my north-end neighbourhood you didn't pop over to visit someone in West Seattle unannounced. Outings there took planning and motivation.

I was preparing to have surgery too, a minor gynaecological procedure to remove small polyps from my uterus. I'd been trying to get pregnant for over a year. Most friends didn't know about the surgery. I'd tell Beth later, teasing her about upstaging me with her bigger, scarier trip to the operating room. But right then, as I steered towards the freeway, I envied the fact that she could tell everyone about what was going on with her body and get the support she needed.

I was jealous of my friend's brain tumour. Fuck.

***

Her operation was successful, the entire tumour removed, but recovery was slow. She spent five weeks in the rehab wing of the hospital regaining her speech and the use of her right leg and hand. After she left the hospital, I kept driving. I worked afternoons and evenings as a librarian, so I could take Beth to her appointments while Kevin went to work. Driving Miss Peterman, we called it.

"Where to, Miss Peterman?" I'd say before pulling away from the curb in front of her house.

It felt nice to have a concrete task after extending that vague offer, "let me know if there's anything I can do to help." On drives, Beth and I filled each other in on things that happened during the time we were out of touch. It was as though one of us lived on a deserted island for a year, and we were simply unable to be in contact. No one said, you should have called me when this was happening. Why didn't you call?

It wasn't the time to bring up the rift in our friendship, to wonder aloud what went wrong. There was no tangible reason for either of us to apologize. Still, it seemed important to acknowledge it, at least to me. *I'm sorry about everything*, I wanted to say, but the words get stuck in my throat. We never did have that conversation, the one where we figured out the reason for our mutual silence. We just moved forward.

There's something about driving that allows for more honesty than sitting face-to-face in a living room or a restaurant. On our drives I felt like we could heal, not just the schism in our relationship, but many of the problems of the world. Maybe not while sitting in city traffic, or dodging construction cones on back streets. But if the drive were long enough, a straight stretch of road through farm country, maybe, or corkscrewing up a mountain road, then we could've gotten down to it.

One day, after Beth's physical therapy appointment, we stopped at a café by the beach for lunch. I was parallel parking when my cell phone rang. The fertility clinic, with results from my latest blood test. Beth retrieved her handicapped parking tag from her bag and hung it on my rear-view mirror. We got out of the car, and as we made our way down the sidewalk to the restaurant, I told Beth the news from the clinic.

"My FSH is low, a three." Before she asked, I translated: follicle-stimulating hormone. It helped determine the age of my eggs.

"Aren't they thirty-two years old, like the rest of you?" she asked. Well, yes, I explained, but FSH regulates the rate at which they mature. High FSH means your eggs are old before their time. Old eggs mean bad odds of fertilization.

"So a three is good," Beth said. "Way to ace the test."

The fertility specialist had made her diagnosis five minutes into our first meeting.

"The problem is scar tissue from your surgery." We knew from an earlier test that my tubes weren't blocked on the inside. "But there might be scar tissue surrounding them, making it so they can't reach up and grab the egg." I had to be reminded of the lesson I'd learnt in seventh grade biology, that fallopian tubes float free at one end like a sea anemone.

Beth and I found a table by the window, and after we ordered, I steered the conversation back to her.

"What am I supposed to do if you have a seizure while you're with me?" She'd been having small ones—petit mals—several times a week since she left the hospital.

"Nothing. Make sure I don't knock my lunch onto the floor. Move the forks out of my reach." She was matter-of-fact, as always, but I still worried. It reminded me of the feeling I had at age seven when my teacher was pregnant. Her entire third trimester, I worried that she would go into labour and I'd have to assist with the birth right there on the playground. Petit mals were normal, Beth said. They were adjusting her medication. She hoped they'd stop soon.

"I'd like to drive again someday," she said. On the board-walk across the street, people travelled parallel to the strip of sand: cycling, jogging, and rollerblading, taking advantage of the rare moment of spring sunshine. Cars passed by the restaurant, and then, a site more commonly seen in summer: a bright-red, six-passenger vehicle with bicycle wheels. It sported a red-and-white striped canopy. A surrey with the fringe on top. I pointed out the window, and Beth turned her head.

"Forget cars," I said. "You can ride around town in style."

"I don't think I could get that thing up the hill to my house," Beth said.

"Not by yourself," I said. "We could take turns."

# 14. Recurrence

One May afternoon I sat in my living room waiting for a phone call from Dr Tom. The previous year, 2003, had been an eventful one with Beth's seizure and her surgery. Though they'd removed the entire tumour, she underwent radiation, just to be sure, acquiring an array of stylish hats to conceal hair loss. She was in remission, with MRIs every three months to detect any recurrence of abnormal cells. She required more sleep than she had pre-tumour, and still wasn't allowed to drive. But life seemed to return to normal for her. We went out to hear music and she went back to work at the foundation. She complained about politicians, her tone a note less cynical than before.

It had been an eventful year for me as well: two in-vitro cycles, the second one resulting in a pregnancy. For six weeks in the spring of 2004 Matt and I woke to a world full of chirping birds and fragrant flowers that seemed to be blooming just for us. We invited friends over to celebrate my thirty-third birthday. I blew out the candles on my cake, my cheeks flushed red with our secret.

The evening of the party, the bleeding began. For over a week it started and stopped, started and stopped. Matt and I made trips to the fertility clinic every few days. The ultrasounds detected a beating heart, the beat slowing, and finally stopping. On the screen, the tiny blob of Matt's and my genetic combination. I had never seen anything so white, or so still.

Matt photocopied the ultrasound photo the doctor gave us. We hiked a river trail in the Snoqualmie Mountains east of Seattle with the copied photo in our backpack. I read words I'd written the night before while Matt tore the paper into shreds. We scattered them into the water and watched while they floated away. In my lifetime, I hadn't felt sadder or more broken: my womb a shrivelled urn, my heart shot full of holes.

\*\*\*

A month later, a too-familiar pain emerged near my tailbone. I went to see Dr Tom. Another CT scan, another wait for results. In my living room that day, I felt physically pain-free. I tried to trick myself into imagining the pain was a false alarm, but I wasn't surprised to hear the graveness of Tom's voice when he called.

"It's back," he said, meaning the teratoma, the tumour that they'd removed five years before. It's back, the phrase indicating an alien invasion, a supernatural being lodged at the bottom of my spine. But my teratoma was one of the most natural parts of my body, a growth that had been there since I was in utero, that came back after they cut it out. Maybe my own foetus had one, too. Maybe they were the reason for the miscarriage, our twin teratomas. Maybe my body was not meant to reproduce.

"A colostomy for sure this time," Dr Tom said, plunking the news down without preamble. The growth sat too low down this time to preserve my colon's function. He thought the teratoma was benign, as before, but they couldn't be sure until the pathologist made his post-surgical pronouncement.

It was too much information to absorb, this phone call

full of devastation. Instead of swelling in the summer months, my abdomen would be cut open. Again. It wasn't a death sentence, a cancer diagnosis, or even a chronic illness. Many people had experienced worse. But I didn't focus on that. All suffering is relative, except to the sufferer.

I looked around my living room. The white gerbera daisies my sister sent after the miscarriage stood in a green glass vase on the mantle. I stroked the arm of the couch, frayed from years as an unofficial cat-scratching post. I'd already rearranged the furniture in my mind to make space for a toy shelf and a rocking chair. Outside the window, pink blossoms weighed down the cherry tree branches. It was late in the day, and Tom seemed eager to get off the phone as soon as the words were out of his mouth.

"We can discuss this further when I see you," he said. Normally a genial man, his tone over the line that day sounded formal, his consonants clipped. I could picture him sitting in his office, the last person left in the clinic at the end of the day. The daylight faded outside the window at his back. He turned in his leather chair as he talked to me, looking out onto the bay and the ferry making its slow crossing. Or perhaps he stood by his desk, one arm already in his coat, reaching across a pile of charts to flick off the lamp as he told me to call back in the morning to make an appointment.

Later, Matt walked through the front door and I told him the news. He sank down on the couch beside me, pulling me into a long hug. We drove through our child-filled neighbourhood to walk on a trail by the lake. His hand held mine in a tight grip as we watched a turtle scramble onto a piece of driftwood in the approaching darkness.

# 15. Trash Can

We scheduled the colostomy surgery for July. I had six weeks to prepare, six weeks to walk around knowing I had a tumour inside of me. Dr Tom and Dr Stan would perform the surgery; we had to wait for Dr Stan to return from his month-long vacation in Greece. I should've been there with him, relaxing on the beach, giving my colon a farewell tour. Instead, I scrambled to make arrangements for a three-month leave from my job as a teen services librarian.

Adolescents spend a lot of idle summer time at the library, and they needed activities to fill the space once their allotted internet time ran out or we'd have a riot on our hands. I set up monthly movie nights, a henna tattoo workshop, a book-reviewing contest. I visited the local schools to promote the library's summer-reading program, and wrote instructions for the librarians who would carry out the tasks that comprised my work days: run the teen book group, process new books, break up fights, un-jam printers, clean graffiti off tables. I worked my shifts at the reference desk, watching patrons enter and exit the library, blithely unaware of my misfortune. Sometimes I tried to see how long I could pretend that I wasn't about to have surgery. It made going to work like performing an eight-hour play.

When I wasn't ticking items off my to-do list, I obsessed about life with a colostomy. This time I felt determined to advocate for myself. I joined an online support group for people with ostomies of different kinds, who called themselves "ostomates." I went through my clothes closet, purging anything that wouldn't conceal my new appliance. And I thought about the form of trash I would soon generate. If my brain were an old-fashioned card catalogue, at any given moment the drawer would be open to the entry that read: *Faeces—Disposal Of.*

I'd met with the hospital's ostomy nurse. I felt better knowing a health care provider existed for the purpose of helping me manage my newly configured intestines. She explained that after my surgery my colon would exit my body at my abdomen, to the left of my navel. I would have a flange—an adhesive disk with a hole in the middle—stuck to my belly. A plastic-lined cloth pouch clipped to the flange. Without a rectal muscle, faeces would empty into the pouch of its own free will. When the pouch was full, I would remove it, bag it up, and throw it away.

"A few months after your surgery, I'll teach you how to irrigate," she told me, a process that would minimize the number of times I had to change the pouch. With irrigation, my solid waste disposal could be kept to a mostly at-home affair. But there would be times when I had to perform the changing task in bathrooms other than my own.

At the library the staff bathroom, a one-seater, sat ten feet from my desk. I realized with a surge of panic that the trash can was problematic: Tall, out of reach of the toilet, no lid. Was a lidless waste basket the best place to throw my bagged-up poop? What about the odour? Colostomies aside, I was a fan of trash-can lids, especially in a bathroom meant to serve a staff of fifty. One morning, determined to assert my needs, I flagged down my co-worker on her way to the break room. Kim was responsible for ordering supplies for our library branch. Three people at work knew about my colostomy: the branch manager, the assistant manager, and Kim.

"Oh," she'd said when I told her my surgery news, like I'd announced I was getting a haircut. "One of my high-school boyfriends had a colostomy. I helped him change it sometimes." I told her I would not require her services myself.

"Can we get a new trash can for the bathroom?" I asked her when she stopped at my desk. "You know, with a lid?" She paused to consider this, and then her eyes lit in acknowledgement.

"I'll go through the office supply catalogue right after my lunch break." Problem solved.

An hour later, Kim returned to my desk. Lidded trash cans, it turned out, cost a lot of money. She had to talk to our assistant manager to approve the charge. The assistant manager was a thoughtful, detail-oriented person. On my first day of work, she brought me a bouquet of flowers for my desk. She specialized in untangling the large knots we often got ourselves into while serving our challenging collection of patrons. Any problem that befell us—a leaky faucet, a rude patron, a difficult research question—she was the first one we called out for. On occasion, she'd been known to over-think a problem. Kim explained why she wanted to buy the new trash can.

"It's for Janet," Kim told her, as though I would get my own special, personalized can. I pictured my name painted in festive script on the side, my photograph pasted to the lid. In their three-minute conversation, the assistant manager thought of several reasons why ordering a lidded trash can would be an inadequate solution. I went to her office.

"It's a bodily fluid," she said, "so it requires special disposal."

"What about tampons and pads?" I asked. "What about diapers?" Technically, she told me, you weren't supposed to throw those into a public receptacle. This was news to me. But, she told me brightly, I had a special need, and the library system had to accommodate me.

"We are required by law," she said. She needed to call the director of human resources. She'd get back to me as soon as possible.

\*\*\*

Two months later my library manager called. Like the assistant manager, she was warm, friendly, and had an easy laugh. Unlike her, the manager did not enjoy dwelling on details. She liked to cross things off her list and move on.

"I hate to bother you," she said, "but I have a list of questions I'm supposed to ask you." I could see her eyes roll through the phone line. She paused. "It's about the fucking trash can."

"You're kidding."

Apparently, the entire Human Resources Department had been on the case of the Trash Can Conundrum. They had a call in to a public health nurse for a consultation. While they awaited her response, they brainstormed solutions. One bright idea, drummed up, no doubt, by the newest employee wanting to make a good impression, involved arranging a special trash pickup just for me. My shit would have its own valet. They wanted to know details in order to facilitate this service: How many times a day would I change the pouch? What kind of bag would it be disposed in?

My manager couldn't believe she had to ask me the questions, and I couldn't believe I had to answer them. But she did, and I did. After I stammered my responses, half-angry, half-laughing, she told me some library gossip to make me feel better, and then we hung up.

I should never have said anything, just thrown my special trash in the open can and not worried about it. Or maybe I should've just gone to Target and bought a lidded trash can myself. I imagined a letter I could've written to the director of Human Resources, full of lies she'd never uncover. *They didn't have to put in a colostomy after all. My shit will go in the toilet just like yours.* I pictured her face turning a deeper shade of red with each word: Colostomy. Shit. Toilet. Then maybe she would understand how it felt to lie on my couch ten miles from her office and envision the staff meetings— I'm sure there were many—in which they discussed my bodily functions.

\*\*\*

One month later, I returned to work. The public health nurse, when reached, politely told the Human Resources folks they were off their rockers. The staff bathroom was outfitted according to her professional recommendations: the same trash can we had before, and, next to the toilet, another, smaller can. With a lid.

# 16. Olympus

Beth phoned a week before my operation.

"I'm taking you on a pre-surgery outing," she said.

"Great," I said. "Where are we going?"

"Olympus. It's a Korean-style women's spa. It's in Tacoma. My treat, but you have to drive." Even in remission, she had to be seizure-free for over a year before she could get behind the wheel again.

"Of course."

We went on a Friday, driving south on the interstate in a heavy rain. We talked about my surgery in the car. It was unclear from my CT scan how large the teratoma was this time, or whether or not other organs were involved. They were considering bringing in a spinal surgeon, maybe a gynaecologist if I ended up needing a hysterectomy. Everyone waited while Dr Tom made his deliberations.

"My sphincter has been in a knot about this all month," he told me. Did he actually refer to his sphincter while talking about removing mine?

Beth and I laughed about this, but I found his comment almost as alarming as the thought of having my uterus and the bottom section of my spine removed. With my first operation, he'd been confident, cocky, even. In the month leading up to my colostomy surgery he was unsure of what to do, and whether or not he could fix me.

At the spa, Beth and I stripped down in the locker room, then got in the hot tub. When I began to overheat, I sat on the edge and dangled my feet in the water. Women of various shapes and ages sat in two large, hot pools. The pool area was ringed with small steam rooms and saunas. Four massage tables lined one wall, and women climbed on and off to receive massages and skin treatments. We all sat naked on large white tiles, bathed in bright fluorescent light. The atmosphere was more industrial than the cedar-and-dim-lighting spas I'd visited in the past. But it was the perfect activity for me that day. Maybe I could sweat away my anxiety.

The anticipation of a second surgery, I'd noticed, was absent of the ignorance I'd had the first time around. This split two ways: less fear, more dread. I knew now what my doctor meant when he told me it would feel like I'd been hit by a truck. I knew that it would take all of my energy to walk a block, that any painkiller stronger than Tylenol 3 would upset my stomach.

Beth and I returned to the locker room for our robes, and I went into a side room to call my surgeon. He still hadn't made any decisions. I went back into the locker room, where Beth sat, taking long sips from her water bottle.

"No news yet," I said. She gave me a look, part sympathetic, part let's-go-kick-that-doctor's-ass.

"Time for some earth energy," she said. We left the locker room, still in our robes, and walked down a narrow hallway to the charcoal-and-sand room. Canvas-covered beach sand, as if wind-blown into tiny dunes, made up the floor of the room. Charcoal blocks lined the walls. It was dry-desert hot, the lighting dim. We lay down on the lumps of sand and breathed in charcoal-laced air. Finally, I felt my body settle into the floor, the knot in my chest loosening with each breath. We were silent for a few minutes. Beth's breathing was deep and even, and I wondered if she'd fallen asleep.

"This is insane," she said quietly.

"The room?" I said.

"No," she said, propping herself up on one elbow. "This. What's happening to you." I turned my head towards her, keeping the rest of my body still.

"You mean how zombies are coming to take my internal organs?"

"Something like that."

"Don't forget about you. They took a bite out of your brain."

"True. But your colon. Your uterus. Maybe part of your spine."

"My uterus isn't doing me much good anyway."

She was right, of course. We were both thirty-three. We weren't supposed to play this caregiver role for many years. Even then, we should have practiced beforehand on our parents. Someone was messing with the natural order of things. We were supposed to be lying on a real beach with our husbands by our sides. Hosting each other's baby showers, and washing our infants in the bathroom sink.

Were we going to go on like this for years, trading illnesses, taking pre-operative spa trips? Bringing by bags of groceries and lasagnes? Once Matt and I had gone with Beth and Kevin on a last-minute trip to Vancouver for the weekend. Now a spontaneous get-together meant that Beth stopped by our house after a dentist appointment. The distance we travelled together, once stretching across the Ecuadorian mountains, now was a circuit from her house to the farmer's market and back. We made the slow laps of the elderly.

"I protest," Beth said in the charcoal-and-sand room, still up on her elbow. "I'm picketing outside the operating room."

"Save Janet's Uterus!"

\*\*\*

Two weeks later I sat with my small entourage in the lounge at one end of the hospital ward where I'd spent the past six days, the same ward I'd stayed on for my two previous surgeries. It was my last night in the hospital; I'd be discharged the following morning. My parents were there, and Matt of course. Beth and Kevin had brought a dinner of sandwiches and salads from the Whole Foods deli, and the six of us talked animatedly as we ate. My appetite was returning already, more quickly than after surgeries one and two.

When Dr Stan returned from Greece the week before, he'd been full of the self-assurance that seemed to have evaporated from Dr Tom's mind. They'd left my uterus in place as well as most of my spine, removing only my coccyx bone because the tumour had entirely surrounded it. I was getting used to the colostomy and had already had my first tutorial in how to change out the entire system for a fresh one.

I didn't have the stamina to participate in the conversation for long, so after a few minutes I stopped talking. As I took slow bites of my sandwich I watched Beth and my father in conversation, both talking fast. She'd been cancer-free for over a year, but it didn't seem like that long before that I'd brought her lunch during her five-week hospital stay. Then, the swelling from her surgery halted her speech, creating long pauses while she struggled to retrieve the words she wanted to say. By the time my surgery arrived, Beth's quarterly MRIs were the main reminder of her former cancer status. I too would move past this acute phase of healing. I'd return to work at the library and adjust to life with my newly configured intestines.

"You'll be the poster child for people with colostomies,"

my manager had said, and I knew she was right. I'd do everything I'd done pre-ostomy, and more.

A nurse walked by the lounge entrance, pausing to smile at us before continuing down the hall. I recognized her as my favourite nurse from my stay five years before. She'd told me funny stories about her kids and brought me blankets straight from the warmer when my fevers spiked. I thought of getting up to call after her, but that would have required more physical effort than I could manage. Besides, I didn't want to disturb the bubble surrounding our group, as though we were gathered around a campfire together, swapping stories and eating food that tasted more delicious than it would back home.

Instead, I chose to linger in the intimate space created by my family and friends. We had a shared understanding, the six of us, of pain, recovery, care giving. I knew from my previous surgeries that the purity of the experience would dissolve once I healed. I wouldn't miss the physical sensations caused by the surgery, of course, the nausea and weakness and the feeling that I'd been struck by a train. But I would miss the raw level of interactions with people, as though a layer of film had been removed from our outer selves. It felt like looking through a window just after the screen has been removed, the clear view in the moment before you notice the dirt streaks.

During Beth's surgery and recovery, the broken thread of our friendship repaired itself. It seemed to be made of a more pliable material than before, better able to withstand inevitable bumps in the road. When my teratoma came back, the thread doubled in strength. Just as married couples possess a shorthand for communicating with one another, Beth and I seemed to be developing a code that we could transmit with a phrase or a knowing smile. The language of our friendship now had a new layer similar to that of platoon-mates. And maybe we were in a way. Not fighting a war, exactly, but writing a survival guide for dwelling in the Kingdom of the Sick.

I took a bite of my sugar cookie, which had the taste of rotting eggs. I grimaced and put it back on my plate. Beth turned her head in time to see my sour expression. She paused her conversation with my father.

"Need something chocolatier?" she said to me.

"Maybe so." She picked up the bar from the table in front of her, snapped off a square, and handed it to me.

"Chocolate is an integral part of the post-surgical diet," she said.

"I couldn't agree more," my father said. The two of them grinned, watching me, and I smiled back. Like physicians, friends and family have bedside manners. We don't stitch up wounds, or clean them. We don't cure. We sit, we listen. We bring food. We eat. It's not enough. But it's what we can do.

I took a bite of the chocolate square and let it melt in my mouth for a moment before I swallowed.

# 17. Waiting Season

For as long as I could remember, I'd wanted to have children. I started babysitting when I was twelve, though I wasn't a natural at caretaking. I accidentally fed diaper cream to my first babysitting charge, thinking it was teething gel, and got fired from another job after a four-year-old broke an antique lamp. But I got better, and babysat or worked at day-care centres until I went to college. I had a vision the whole time of my own offspring: two kids who looked the way that I did in childhood photographs, blue-eyed, curly-haired. Jam smeared on their faces, and dried leaves in their hair after they raked a pile, then jumped in.

***

Of course, those childhood fantasies assumed I'd have no trouble producing offspring. Back at the beginning of our fertility clinic visits, Matt and I talked about adoption. In those days it felt to us like the last stop on a long train ride, the unfamiliar city people visit only when the tourist-town hotels are all full. Once the treatments began to fail, though, we reconsidered our stance. When my teratoma came back, I became concerned about passing along my genetic material. Maybe the biological route was not the best option. but Matt and I decided that, above all, we wanted to be parents. The particulars of how we arrived there began to seem less important.

In the months following my colostomy surgery I read

books about adoption and Matt and I attended seminars given by attorneys and adoptive parents. We had many decisions to make: international versus domestic, private or through the foster care system. We learnt about open adoption, where birth parents chose the adoptive families and together created an agreement for ongoing contact.

"We meet our son's birthmom at the zoo, or the park," one woman said at a panel discussion we attended. Before the adoption, she told us, their friends and family worried that an open adoption would be confusing for their child.

"It's only confusing for adults," she said. "For our son, it's simply more people in his life who love him."

"I could do meet-ups at the zoo," Matt said in the car on the way home. "I love the zoo." We began to imagine the get-togethers we'd have with our child's birth family: canoe trips and visits to the mountains together to go hiking or sledding.

"What if the birthparents aren't outdoorsy?" I said.

"Then we'll go to the science museum," Matt said. "We'll go to the mall."

"The mall? You hate the mall."

"If our kid's birthmom wanted to go to the mall, I'd go to the mall."

We found an agency we liked, and filled out heaps of paperwork. Then we waited. All those hours logged at clinics, staring at lobby fish tanks and perched at the edge of exam tables drained me of patience and an ability to sit still. The adoption timeline was uncertain, and in the meantime, I needed to move.

First, I quit my job. My fantasies about being a librarian had been filled with scenes of converting teenaged book-haters into book-lovers and arming immigrants with ESL and citizenship test materials. Some days included those activities, but they were few and far between. More often I found myself un-jamming printers and filling out incident reports on belligerent patrons I'd had to ban from the library. I thought I was working for an organization that was the hallmark of a democratic society, providing free and open access to materials that would improve people's lives. But it felt more like working at Kinko's.

"Lucky you," said one co-worker at my going away party. "No job, no responsibilities at home. You're a free agent."

"So jealous," said another. I did not say that I'd suppressed my own envy for years as I listened to them discussing Girl Scout meetings, little league games, describing their weekends spent crowding around a popcorn bowl on their too-small couches for family movie nights.

If I wasn't a librarian or a Mom, what was I? A waiter, but not the kind that works in a restaurant and gets tips. I got headaches from grinding my teeth in my sleep. I tried to will the phone to ring, a call from our adoption agency telling us we'd been chosen to parent a baby.

They did call, several times. Matt and I would spend the ensuing hours or days mapping out various scenarios for our about-to-drastically-change family structure. Then another phone call would come, the social worker apologetic, to tell us it was over. Again and again, the "maybe" scenarios went sideways. The mom decided to parent the baby, or a grandparent stepped in, or someone else.

"I hope we call with better news soon," the social workers always said. We'd limp through the next few days, exhausted, until the world recalibrated itself around us. The months crawled by until, finally, I had to do something drastic. I came up with the most rash gesture I could conjure. I registered for a triathlon.

Preparing for a race sounded like the antithesis of fertility treatments, my body always in motion as I toned my muscles and soaked my t-shirts with sweat. The schedule was full of the certainty I craved: On Monday, bike eight miles. On Tuesday, laps in the swimming pool for forty minutes. Maybe it would feel like the endorphin-filled days in college when I tried out for the ski team, this exercising with a purpose and a goal. I also liked the idea of being able to circle a date on the calendar. My friends all marked their datebooks with their babies' due dates. I could have a big day of my own: Race Day.

I registered for the Danskin Triathlon, an all-women's sprint-distance race held in late summer. A half-mile swim in Lake Washington, a twelve-and-a-half mile bike ride up the boulevard and onto the express lanes of Interstate 90. The finish line for the three-mile run sat a few hundred feet from the beach where the whole thing began. I'd stood at that finish line once, watching a friend run across. She'd delivered her second baby less than two months before. If she could complete the race, I could too.

***

I was late to the triathlon craze. The first modern-day triathlon was held in San Diego in 1974. One evening in September, forty-six people toed the starting line in a run-swim-bike-swim event. The final swimmers completed the event with car headlights illuminating the course, and the entire group went out for pizza afterwards. Among the racers were John and Judy Collins, who would go on to organize the first Ironman triathlon in Hawaii a few years later.

In 1990, when I was in college, Danskin held its first women's triathlon, the same year they expanded their dancewear line to include athletic apparel. By 2006, over two million people were competing in triathlons each year, many of them women. Danskin had professional triathlete Sally Edwards as its spokesperson, who helped beckon first-timers by creating the most beginner-friendly race of its kind. If you feared swimming in open water, you could request a "swim angel" to follow you, towing a foam noodle that you could stop and hold onto if needed. Sally Edwards did every race, bringing up the rear so that no participant had to be the last to finish. Every participant got a medal, a tarnished gold disc hung from a purple nylon lanyard. On the back, in smile-shaped letters it read *the woman who starts the race is not the same woman who finishes the race.*

I bought a book, *Triathlons 101*, which provided a training schedule and advised me on nutrition and equipment. The author advised taking time to visualize ourselves at each stage of the race, completing one leg and transitioning to the next. I was supposed to imagine myself crossing the finish line, running strong until both feet were on the other side. I pictured Matt standing at the edge of the nylon barricade, a baby strapped to his front. Our baby. In my fantasy, Matt picked up the baby's arm, made the baby wave. The baby smiled at me, and thought the word she could not yet say: *Mama.*

\*\*\*

Summer training meant a first for me and Matt: bringing our bicycles on vacation. We drove to Missoula where Matt led a seminar at a civil engineering conference. I rode my bike around Missoula's foothills while Matt sat in over-air conditioned meeting rooms. We spent our evenings outside, at the minor league baseball game, or eating over-sized sandwiches at the outdoor tables of a local pub. At the farmer's market one afternoon, I spotted a flyer for an outdoor community concert. It didn't identify the band by name; I pictured a group of local undergrads.

We arrived at the park at dusk. Children filled the storybook scene, just as they did back in Seattle: zooming down the playground slide, splashing in the fountain, riding in strollers between their parents, the family dog trotting alongside. A sea of tanned, happy faces spread blankets on the wide lawn.

Matt and I claimed an empty square of grass. I plunked down and took out my yarn. A few years before, my mom had taught me how to knit, and I worked on my second-ever knitting project, a baby blanket in a patchwork of differently-coloured squares. Once this was finished, I'd knit a larger version for the expectant parents who chose us, whomever they would be. Friends would knit some of the squares, mailing them to me when finished, a long-distance quilting bee of sorts.

"How many squares are you up to?" Matt asked as propped himself up on his elbow, legs bent to fit in the small patch of unoccupied lawn. The mom next to us unpacked a picnic supper, ladling potato salad onto paper plates while the Dad chased their meandering toddler, trying to entice her back to their blanket with the promise of lemonade and chocolate chip cookies.

"This will be number three, for lavender," I said, plunging my fingers into the downy ball of yarn. A group of two dozen retirees mounted the bandstand steps. They were dressed in white button-downs, with cherry scarves for the women, matching bolo ties for the men. The local senior choir.

"A college band, huh?" Matt said, laughing.

"My mistake," I said. We decided to stay. What else was

there to do that evening, anyway? I zipped up my fleece jacket as the sun sank behind the mountain. The choir began to sing. I looked up at Mount Sentinel. I'd tried to run up the trail that afternoon, but it was too steep for me, and I'd turned around after a few hundred feet. At the top of the trail sat a hundred-foot tall concrete M, stark white against the brown hillside. M for Miscarriage. M for Motherhood. M for Maybe someday.

# 18. Caleb

Over a year after we completed our adoption paperwork, we got picked. Bree, age twenty-four, lived in a small coastal town in southern Washington with her six-year-old, Sam. Bree liked the fact that we weren't religious, and both she and Sam were happy about the fact that we liked spending time outdoors.

"When I was looking at the letters and photos, I kept coming back to yours," Bree told us the first time she met us, at a playground next to the hospital where she was scheduled to deliver. "I had this familiar feeling, like I'd met you before."

I didn't share that familiar feeling. All I felt when I was with Bree was a sense of awe and wonder—who was this woman who was getting ready to deliver a baby and then give him or her to Matt and me to raise? I wasn't sure how well we would get to know each other before the birth. Our homes were nearly four hours apart, making get-togethers challenging. Bree was shy, and in my nervousness I produced a constant chatter whenever we were together. I hadn't yet adjusted to the unfamiliar nature of our relationship, like the American equivalent of an arranged marriage. By necessity we'd skipped the small-talk phase to discuss things like birth plans, future visits, and our legally binding adoption plan.

We needed to discuss names. Though no one knew the baby's sex, we all operated under the assumption that it would be a boy. Matt and I had long-ago chosen Caleb, the only boy's name we both liked.

"Would you like to choose the middle name?" we asked Bree over the phone.

"How about if you give me a list and we pick together?"

We visited their little town one Saturday a few weeks before Bree's due date. After having a picnic lunch and flying kites in a drizzle, we went to a coffee shop, where Bree would not let us pay for her and Sam's hot cocoa. I pulled our list of names out of my bag and slid it across the table. Sam looked down.

"Evan," he said, pointing, a smile on his face.

"You like that one?" Bree asked him. "It's like our last name, isn't it?"

"What's your last name?" Matt asked. We'd only been given each other's first names.

"Evans." Matt and I looked at each other, then at Sam and Bree.

"That's a pretty big coincidence," Matt said.

"I think we found our name," I said.

***

There was a father, of course. John. He had red hair, Bree told us, and worked at his Dad's construction company. Bree and John were no longer a couple, but he knew about the adoption plan. He said he'd sign the papers, but had yet to do so. He was struggling with the decision, Bree told us. He didn't return the counsellor's phone calls.

When our adoption was a hypothetical event in the future, our family and friends seemed to want to apply generalities. We'd had to dispel a lot of myths—no, it wasn't mostly teenagers who chose adoption. No, birthmoms weren't all alcoholics and drug addicts. They weren't all anything, except women with unplanned pregnancies.

Once Bree chose us, though, and the hypothetical became more real, Matt and I clung to tidbits of information gleaned from the two-day training on open adoption the agency had required us to take when we started the process two years before. One counsellor had said that birth parents who've already parented other children, like Bree, are less likely to change their minds. They already know how hard the job is. Bree and Sam's father divorced when Sam was two, and Bree had been his sole caretaker ever since.

"I don't want to take away from the little that Sam has," she told us. She'd been planning the adoption since she was two months pregnant. She's unlikely to change her mind became our mantra.

At the same time, the looming fear was, of course, that Bree or John would change their minds. It was their right. Nothing got legally cemented until a court hearing to terminate parental rights, which would happen forty-eight hours after the birth. This was short relative to most states, but still felt like an eternity. It was hard to imagine how I would keep my heart in the limbo place it had resided in for years once I'd held the baby, named him, fed him.

\*\*\*

In mid-June Matt and I drove south to spend the night at a Travelodge near the hospital in Longview, Washington where Bree was scheduled to deliver. She would have an induction the following morning, and she'd invited us to be in the delivery room for the birth.

"I have to check into the hospital at 6:00 a.m.," Bree told me on the phone a few days beforehand.

"We'll meet you at the registration desk," I said.

The evening before the birth, Matt and I pulled into the hotel parking lot and carried our bags from the car to our room. We'd brought a cooler full of food intended for a supper by the narrow lake across the street from the hospital. Angry clouds hovered above the city, though, sending down occasional raindrops.

"Let's have a hotel room picnic," I said.

Matt lay towels down on top of the nylon bedspread while I removed Tupperware lids and retrieved plastic dishes from one of our backpacks. Another pack held our camera and books, magazines, crossword puzzles to entertain us at the hospital while Bree was in labour. A third bag contained items for the day we'd bring the baby home. I'd packed three sets of pajamas, hoping Bree would choose the baby's first outfit.

We had the baby blanket I'd knit, plus the larger one that friends had contributed to. I'd taught Matt to knit and we'd spent the past few weeks stitching the squares together. We'd made a Certificate of Big Brotherhood to present to Sam at the hospital, and written a letter to Bree to read to her before we parted ways. It had been the most difficult letter I'd ever written, full of inadequate phrases like "we are honoured" and "thank you."

I laid our dinner out on the bed, items we'd prepared at home the night before: pasta with grilled chicken, green beans with basil and balsamic vinaigrette, potato salad. We had grapes and Oreos, beer for Matt and lemonade for me. We'd brought DVDs for the hospital too, trying to guess which ones from our collection Sam might like.

In the hotel room, Matt fiddled with the DVD player and then settled onto the bed next to me. We ladled food onto our plates as familiar music emitted from the speakers. *The Princess Bride*. I smiled.

"My favourite," I said. "How did you know?"

\*\*\*

For the time being Matt's and my statuses remained Not-Mom and Not-Dad. Soon, in a single moment we would switch roles with Bree and John, Matt and I receiving the baby, taking him home, becoming his parents. Bree would release him to our care. Matt and I wouldn't ever get to say *I made him. He came from me.* All of us missing something, the same thing, really, not getting to parent our biological child. But the timing felt all wrong, with Bree's period of sorrow—and John's, even in his absence—becoming Matt's and my time of joy as we won the ultimate prize: having Caleb as our son.

The brink I teetered on felt almost physically real, the event that would change our lives forever happening mere hours from now and only a mile away from the hotel bed where we sat. It felt as though I'd been fishing during this long wait. Each day I unspooled my past sorrows of ill health, infertility, pregnancy loss and reeled in my fears – that there would be something wrong with the baby, that the adoption wouldn't go through. Was I fortunate or un-fortunate, a person bad things happened to or not? I was slowly learning I could be both and neither, that I had to let go of control and accept uncertainty in its place.

\*\*\*

The movie ended. It was 9:30, not yet fully dark. Matt pulled the curtains and I went to the bathroom to get ready for bed. Every action felt laden: last night-time tooth brushing before the baby arrives. Next time I put on these pyjamas, I'll be a Mom. I didn't feel tired, but I still had hopes of getting one more good night of sleep.

"Last uninterrupted slumber for who knows how long," I said to Matt as we climbed into bed.

"You ready?" he said. I was more than ready, I thought. No more longing looks at women pushing strollers up the sidewalk past my house, no more sadness on Halloween, or Christmas, or every single holiday that seemed to be a cruel reminder of my Not-Mom role. The hole in my heart was about to be sewn shut. Motherhood would have its challenges, I knew, but I had no idea of the ways in which its difficulty would bring my insecurities to the surface, or even flatten me. I had no inkling of the moments, fleeting though they would be, when I would miss the time when it was just Matt and me and our picnic basket. I took a deep breath and smiled at Matt.

"I'm ready."

\*\*\*

Less than forty-eight hours later I sat in a chair in Bree's hospital room, watching her as she packed to go home. Caleb, recently fed and changed, slept in a hospital-issue bassinet next to the bed. Sam was with Bree's mom getting food from the hospital cafeteria; Matt had gone down to the parking garage to get something out of our car.

It seemed as though nearly every emotion possible had flooded my system during the previous day and a half, passing through my body like a series of brief but powerful thundershowers. Bree delivered Caleb less than two hours after her first and only dose of Pitocin to induce labour. Halfway out of the birth canal, his hand whipped up to his cheek in a self-soothing gesture. The one ultrasound photo we had displayed his hand on the same cheek, and I imagined his hand had been there during his entire uterine stay.

During our adoption wait I'd told myself I could keep my guard up until the baby was legally ours. But that resolution dissolved the moment Caleb touched his face, before I'd even done so myself.

As we awaited the hospital discharge papers, a new sensation rose in my chest: Panic. Were they really going to send Caleb home with Matt and me? We'd read parenting books, taken an infant care class, and observed our friends taking care of their kids. But a newborn? We had no clue what to do. Caleb was so tiny. So helpless. It took confidence to be a parent, I realized. Confidence I wasn't sure I had.

"We need to schedule an appointment for Caleb before we can discharge him," the nurse told me. "Do you have a paediatrician?"

"We do," I said and retrieved a slip of paper from my wallet with the name and phone number of Dr Allen, a paediatrician in Seattle. We'd met with him early in our adoption wait, on the recommendation of my own doctor.

"He's great," she told me. "And very popular. Get in as soon as you can." Nearly a year had passed since our meeting, and he was no longer taking new patients, but our original appointment had secured us a spot. As soon as we'd been picked, I phoned to tell him the due date.

"Congratulations," he said. "I'll leave a note at the front desk so they know you're legit."

***

The O.B. nurse came into Bree's room, her brow furrowed.

"I tried to make you an appointment," she said. "They said you're not in their records." My stomach dropped.

"I'll call," I said, reaching for the slip of paper with the phone number. I looked over at Bree, who was filling out hospital paperwork, a process that clearly frustrated her. She looked up at me and I gave her what I hoped looked like a sympathetic smile.

"Red tape is so much fun, huh?" I said. She gave a half-smile in return. I fished my cell phone out of my pack and dialled the clinic. It was late afternoon, a time, I'd learn later, when the phones rang constantly with calls from panicked parents needing to get medical questions answered and appointments made before the business day concluded. The woman who answered sounded like she didn't have time to talk to me. I swallowed hard and explained the situation – the need to make an appointment before we left the hospital, the previous meeting with the doctor who'd assured us we could have him as our son's paediatrician.

"He said he'd leave a note," I ended lamely. It seemed like we'd need a sworn affidavit to get past the receptionist.

"There's no note," she said. "He's not taking new patients."

"We're not new patients," I said, a fact though it felt like a lie. Caleb was one day old. What else was he besides new? The receptionist pushed an irritated breath through the phone line.

"When did you say you wanted to come in?"

"On Thursday."

"Thursday is his day off," she said, more brightly, "I can schedule you with another physician." But I didn't want another physician. I wanted the popular doctor, the one I'd chosen and met with a year before. In a process that required me to be flexible and keep my expectations in check, choosing a paediatrician had been one of the only things I'd allowed myself to plan and count on. The frustration I'd spent the previous ten years tamping down uncoiled inside of me. The universe owed me Dr Allen. I wouldn't back down.

We went back and forth, finally settling on Wednesday, though the receptionist bristled at this. "We don't normally see two-day-old babies unless there's a health problem. And his schedule is very full."

"I appreciate your fitting us in," I said, trying to return to the kind tone with which I'd started. She told me the appointment time and that I'd need to arrive fifteen minutes early to fill out paperwork. I thanked her and hung up the phone, sinking into a chair and letting all of my breath out at once.

The biggest emotions of the day would come later, when we held a goodbye ceremony in the hospital room. We'd already scheduled a phone call for the following week, and had plans for a visit later in the summer. The adoption counsellor would facilitate the ceremony, inviting Bree's mom and Sam into the room to stand beside Bree as she sat on the bed with Caleb in her arms. Matt and I would give the blanket we'd made to Bree, and present Sam with his Certificate of Big Brotherhood. I'd read Bree the letter I'd written weeks before.

Everyone except for Sam and Caleb would cry. Matt would buckle Caleb into his car seat and carry him out of the room. I would trail after them, leaving Bree to sob into her mom's shoulder. I'd envisioned the scene for weeks, my stomach in a knot. It would be far more wrenching than I'd imagined.

It wouldn't be until much later that I'd feel the triumph of the phone call to the paediatrician's office. I didn't know then that part of being a parent meant advocating for your child frequently from age zero onward. That this near-constant state of assertion would make it easier for me to stand up for myself in some settings, but not others. But the fact remained that, on my first full day as a mom, I'd asserted myself at last.

# 19. Cancerversary

I did not hear the phone ring.

I stood in the shower, post-scrubbing, letting the water run over my already-tightening muscles. It was August 2008, a year after Caleb was born, and that morning I'd completed my second triathlon. I felt the satisfying kind of tired that accompanies the immediate aftermath of a race. I allowed my mind a decadent thought: I have everything I want. Life is good.

My first year of momhood had been the blissful experience I'd fantasized about all those years of my illness and infertility, the one I felt I was due. Caleb had been an easy baby, laughing easily and sleeping through the night at the age of four months. By the time his first birthday arrived his high-octane personality had revealed itself. He went from crawling to walking to running in a rapid-fire developmental progression, and his body rarely remained still when he was awake. In music class, the parents sat in a circle, their children in their laps, tapping softly on miniature drums. During class my lap remained empty while Caleb ran laps around the circle's perimeter. At the playground, Matt and I took turns in the role of spotter while Caleb climbed out of our reach on the jungle gym.

Apparently, though, I didn't feel busy enough. We'd met with architects to plan a house remodel and recently turned in paperwork to our agency to adopt a second child. How another baby would fit into our lives, I wasn't entirely sure.

Parenting Caleb consumed all of our time, and then some. But it seemed like a given that we would have two children. It was the image I'd conjured for myself since childhood, and the one that persisted in the many parenthood-themed conversations with Matt over the years.

"We need two," I said, "so they can play together. They'll be best friends."

"Yeah," Matt said, "and two can do all of the housework more easily than one."

Adopting one child had been all about fulfilling our needs to be parents. We thought about a second with Caleb at the forefront of our minds. We wanted the moon for him. It felt essential to his childhood to provide him with a lifelong companion to discover the world alongside.

We didn't have the known timeline that pregnancy provided, a fact that I found frustrating even though it was unchangeable. I pretended not to be attached to any particular age gap, but I secretly harboured a wish for children three years apart. That way Caleb would be already toilet trained and somewhat responsive to verbal instructions by the time the baby arrived.

*** 

I emerged from the bathroom and found Matt at the dining room table, bathed in sunlight, the phone pressed to his ear. He looked up when I approached, an expression on his face that I'd seen too many times before. Beth, he mouthed to me. He did not have to say more. At a pause in the conversation, he told her I was out of the shower, then handed me the phone.

"It's baaack," Beth said, Poltergeist-style, her voice unnaturally high. The room tilted sideways for a split second.

I lowered myself onto our couch, the place in our house I sat to receive bad news, which always seemed to arrive by telephone. The call about my own tumour recurrence was the bottom. But this was worse. Mine: benign. Beth's: malignant.

"Actually, not *it*," she said. "They."

Two tumours this time, each smaller than the original. They sat in the same part of her brain, near her language centre. I remembered how swelling from the first surgery caused long pauses in her speech as she cast about for the word she wanted. On the phone, I searched for the right thing to say. I didn't find it.

"Oh, Beth," I said, my voice a whisper. "Fuck."

\*\*\*

Not long before, Beth had passed the five-year mark, that triumphant milestone for cancer survivors. She sent an email to friends, "happy cancerversary to me!"

"We should have another party," I wrote back. A few months after her first surgery, Matt and I hosted a Beth dinner at our house featuring all of Beth's favourites: grilled halibut, a bean and tofu stir-fry Matt invented called "black bean-y." One friend brought roasted red pepper relish, another brownies swirled with caramel. We dined on our deck and toasted Beth's health as the sun dropped below our neighbours' roofs.

Five years later, though, we had Caleb: toddler, energizer bunny, plan-delayer. Months had gone by since she'd cleared the five-year hurdle and I'd made my party offer. And then, at her very next MRI, white marks on the image.

"Definitely chemo," Beth said. "Maybe surgery. I have to go back to my neuro-oncologist next week." The leaf-laden dogwood branches stretched across my dining room window frame. The unbidden sun that sent shimmers across the lake during my race seemed, from my position on the couch, taunting and cruel.

Beth's voice returned to its confident tone, her sentences drawn out in explanation. She wanted to stop talking about herself.

"Tell me about your race," she said.

"I met someone cool. You'd like her." I'd encountered a teenage girl during the run, and we ran together for a few minutes. She told me she was excited about showing up at school the following week thirty pounds lighter than she'd been the previous spring. She was short and her uneven strides jostled her camelback backpack as she ran. The tie was coming loose on her ponytail, and strands of black hair adhered to the back of her neck. We ran together across a field, complaining about the hot sun as the overgrown grass nipped our ankles. She told me she couldn't wait to see the looks on the girls' faces who'd teased her for being fat. I could picture her standing in the hallway on the first day of school in a new blouse, short-sleeved to show off her newly-defined arms. The other students' voices would still as, one by one, they saw her. And she would say nothing, just smile and walk past.

"Teenage girls are so supportive of each other, aren't they?" Beth said on the phone. She emitted a chuckle usually reserved for responding to Matt's jokes, whether or not they were funny. Not a full laugh, but a sincere one. The distraction was working.

"Go on," she said, "tell me more." So I continued talking. For Beth, I would always have another story.

# 20. Lavawoman

By the time the day of Beth's operation arrived, the two tumours had grown together and the doctor had not been able to get the entire growth out. Surgeons always hope for "clean margins," in tumour-speak. In the brain, though, no such luxuries exist. No margins at all. Their best hope, Kevin told me, was a long course of chemo.

"To get rid of the rest of the growth," I said.

"No," Kevin said in his gentle tone. "To keep it from growing."

\*\*\*

I phoned Beth a few weeks after she got home from the hospital to tell her about an uncharacteristically impulsive decision I'd made. Over-cramming my schedule had become a habit ever since the adoption wait, where time stretched itself wide as a chasm across my days. Even though I was busy being a Mum, that was not all I wanted to be. The only way to have more was to become busier.

"I just signed up to do a triathlon in Hawaii," I told Beth. "Olympic distance. It's called Lavaman."

"Lavaman?" Beth said. "Why man? Why not Lavawoman?"

"I think it's after Ironman. But I like Lavawoman better."

"Let's re-name it," she said.

"Let's." She asked me the distance and I told her: one mile swim, twenty-five mile bike, six point two mile run."

"Wow," she said. "I wish I could do the race vicariously

through you."

"You can," I said. "That's why I was calling. I thought I would do it in your honour, if that's okay with you." I paused, nervous. Would she be insulted? Don't do anything in my honour, I could hear her saying. I'm not dead yet.

"Sounds great," she said.

"Really?"

"Yeah, I mean, you're insane, but you're the good kind of crazy. The kind that still gets invited over for dinner."

I told Beth what I'd learnt from a friend a few days before. I'd be doing the race with Team in Training, the fundraising arm of the Leukaemia and Lymphoma Society. You signed up to train for a race—a triathlon, a marathon, a hundred-mile bike ride. You raised money for LLS, and in turn they provided you with coaches and a training group. They paid your plane fare, hotel, race entry fee.

"With Team in Training," my friend told me, "you can race in honour of a cancer patient. Not just blood cancer. Any kind of cancer."

And there it was: my reason. Beth. Ever since she'd phoned to tell me her cancer had returned, I'd been extending that vague offer, "let me know if there's anything I can do to help." Doing a triathlon wouldn't benefit Beth, not exactly. But at least it was something to do, a way to erode the helpless feeling.

"Picture me strong and healthy," Beth had written in the letter she sent to friends before her surgery, "so that I may return to that state soon." I could visualize Beth as my training partner, maybe, though she hadn't ever been a runner or a strong swimmer, nor did she own a bike. Before she moved to Ecuador she belonged to the gym where I was still a member. More than once we'd returned home together without working out when we couldn't find parking close enough to avoid walking far in the rain. Beth preferred exercising in nature: hiking, kayaking, snowshoeing. While my feet pounded the gym's rubber treadmill I could call up an actual image stored in my photo album: Beth and I hiking at Mount Rainier back before either of us was sick, the mountain a snowy, sun-drenched dome behind us.

\*\*\*

My Team in Training group gathered in the grass at the edge of the track at dusk for our first running practice. We lay jackets and water bottles under the cedar tree canopy and watched a group of men playing soccer on the field in the middle of the track. Light poles half the length of the track itself ringed the outer edge, casting the field's artificial turf in a neon-green light.

I surveyed the group as they chatted, stretched, strapped on heart rate monitors and switched their sports watches to timer mode. At thirty-seven I stood smack in the middle of the group age-wise, and I was the only person on the team with a child under the age of five. I recognized a few people from the kickoff party a few days before. Though we'd race as individuals, we trained as the Lavaman Team.

The team captain, Ande, a bald, chiselled man in his late thirties with biceps bigger than my thighs, laced up a pair of fluorescent running shoes. He looked like the poster boy for Team in Training, but he wasn't. The type of person they hoped to attract was represented in the rest of the group at the track: first-timers, everyday athletes, couch potatoes wanting to change their ways. People who'd seen their friends and family survive cancer, or not.

I wore a new shirt, new sports bra, new running tights, all purchased at Title Nine Sporting Goods Store the previous week. Then, standing in the dressing room, I'd felt like an athlete. At the track, I felt more like an interloper. A poser. I couldn't possibly complete an Olympic-distance triathlon. What was I doing there?

Ande wolf-whistled and we stopped our chatting and gathered around him. Our coach stepped to the front of the group, a short-haired, short-statured woman dressed in black track pants and a navy blue jacket with a fleece lining. She began speaking, her voice quiet, as though she needed to preserve it for a singing gig later that evening. She explained that we would be doing heart-rate testing.

"We want to establish what your heart rates should be at various levels of exertion," she said. The training plan was divided into stages, and required different levels of intensity for workouts at each phase. She gave us the instructions: Run one lap at a slow speed, the next lap at a moderate speed, the last lap fast. She would record our times. She led us in a group stretch, explaining that, before exercise, our stretches should be dynamic.

"Save your static stretches for after your workout," she said, the first time I'd heard this piece of athlete wisdom. Standing near the back of the group, I felt like the oddball Mallard in a group of ducklings, the one who swam out of formation and splashed haphazardly while the others dove smoothly, according to instinct. I re-adjusted my baseball cap on my head three times in a row, pulling it off, sweeping my hair to the back of my head, putting it back on. Try not to trip over your shoelaces, Janet.

The coach blew her whistle and we began to run. I fell into step beside a long-legged man in his twenties. We introduced ourselves. During our slow lap I learnt that Lavaman would be his first triathlon. The bike portion presented the biggest challenge for us both.

GUTS

"I don't even have a road bike," he told me.

"Me neither," I said. "Mine is a hybrid. I'm a really slow rider."

"Is the bike heavy?" he asked.

"Very."

"Then it's the bike's fault," he said, and we laughed.

On the second lap, we picked up the pace as instructed, and talked about our reasons for signing up with Team in Training. I would have this conversation dozens of times in the ensuing months, with teammates, friends, family, strangers. But I didn't have my sound bite yet. I rambled. I told him about my desire to be in good shape, to achieve a fitness goal.

"What's your connection to blood cancer?" he asked.

"My grandfather died of leukaemia when he was forty-four. I have a friend with brain cancer," I said, almost as an afterthought. "She just had surgery." He made a little noise in the back of his throat, the most sympathetic sound you can make while running at a moderate pace. During our conversation we'd passed several people, including chiselled Ande. Why was everyone else still running slowly on the moderate lap? My running companion and I weren't sure. I asked him if he knew anyone with cancer. His pace slowed, but the shift was so subtle I almost didn't notice it.

"My cousin has lymphoma," he said. I'd recently learnt about the two types of lymphoma, Hodgkin's and Non-Hodgkin's. The former is considered a "good" kind of cancer with a high survival rate. The latter is the bad kind. He looked straight ahead, so I couldn't see his eyes to gauge which type his cousin had.

"I'm sorry," I told the side of his face. We passed the tree, our coach, the woman from the Team in Training office. Last lap. Time to speed up. He turned to look at me.

"Thank you," he said. "Tell me your name again."

"Janet."

"It was nice talking to you, Janet." He told me he was going to do the last lap very fast, and then he took off. I accelerated too, more moderately. Everyone was spread out around the track in groups of two or three, some running alone like me. It was impossible to tell who was on what lap, and I felt less like part of a team training for a race, more like an individual out for an evening run.

As I rounded the first arc of the track, the overhead lights went out.

"They only keep them on for the soccer games," our coach would tell us a few weeks later when, soccer season over, she announced that, from now on, we'd run in the dark. Passing cars' headlights created shadows of the branches that overhung the track. Maple leaves formed a carpet runner, their oranges and purples dissolved into tan husks. My right foot struck leaves with each step, my left one packed dirt, each stride a different sensation under the sole of my running shoe. It felt strange and oddly thrilling to begin something new at a time of year when nature folds into itself and all beings prepare for winter.

I rounded the far arc of the track, almost at a sprint, then stopped by the tree. I told the coach my time, breathing hard, bending down to fetch my water bottle from its spot on the grass. She wrote the number I told her down on her clipboard. And then we figured it out. She had given incorrect instructions. She said "lap" when she meant "mile." We were supposed to do one slow mile, one moderate mile, one fast mile. I'd done three laps of a quarter-mile each at slow, moderate, and fast paces. She told me to run two miles at moderate speed.

"Sorry," she said. "You can re-test next week." I ran slowly, no longer noticing the crunch of the leaves. People passed me in pairs, friends from last year's race or ones who'd decided to do their first triathlon together.

I thought of the playlists I'd put on my iPod; The English Beat, The Clash, Michelle Shocked always accompanied me on my runs. Assuming I'd be running in a group, I'd left the iPod at home. My house sat a mile from the track. I could've veered right and gone through the gate, kept running until I reached my front door. I looked at my watch. Caleb would be asleep. I could sit at the dining room table and talk to Matt while I ate dinner. Would anyone even notice I'd gone?

I kept running, of course. I always stuck it out. In college, I never dropped a class. I stayed with a gastroenterologist I didn't like and took pills I didn't want to take. Then I signed up for a triathlon, trying something new even though parenthood was new enough to give me my fill of Things I Don't Know How To Do. Even though Team in Training expected people to drop out, built it into the budget, even, I knew I never would. Once I filled out the registration form, I was on a nonstop flight to Hawaii. Unless I was sick, or out of town, I'd come to every practice. And I'd never, ever, leave in the middle.

\*\*\*

As planned, I joined some teammates for pizza after I finished my last lap. Our fifty-person Lavaman team was subdivided into smaller groups, each with two mentors to help us keep up with fundraising and training. The waiter brought bottles of San Pellegrino, local beer, red wine served in short juice glasses. I ordered an individual pizza with an extra portion of sausage.

"Double meat," my mentor said from across the table. "Good for you, Janet." He passed his cell phone around the table, showing us a photo of his son and daughter. "Spitting images of me, don't you think?" he said. He laughed. He was doughy in body shape and complexion, with pale blue eyes and spiky blonde hair. Two Asian kids, arm in arm, grinned on the tiny screen.

"They have your smile," I said. I told him Caleb was adopted, too.

"My son was adopted," my other mentor said. "We're Team Adoption!" I told her that Matt and I had recently turned in our adoption paperwork.

"What will you do if you get a baby in March?" she asked. It was an important question. Lavaman would take place at the end of March.

"I doubt it will happen that fast."

Of course, I had no idea how long it would take. The person who would choose us could come along in twenty-four hours, in three years, or anytime in between. Someone could've been reading our letter right then, while I ate pizza. Maybe no one would pick us, ever. At that point, it was out of our hands.

When the pizza arrived, I turned to talk to the other side of the table. The woman sitting next to me told me she was an oncology nurse in Tacoma. I assumed she was doing Team in Training because of her work connection, but then she said that her brother had leukaemia.

"He was admitted last week to the hospital where I work," she said. "He's not doing well." I did not yet know that this was code for dying, that I would use the same phrase myself to describe Beth's condition in less than a year. Her brother would be dead within the month, and the cousin of the man I ran with too. Having a loved one die while you were training for a race in their honour seemed like the universe's equivalent of pouring salt in a deep wound.

It was 10:30 by the time we left the restaurant. I lingered on the sidewalk, almost too tired to climb into my own car and drive the half-mile up the hill to my house and collapse into bed beside Matt, already asleep. My new teammates, too, rearranged their personal schedules to fit in training. I thought of their relatives, the cousin of the man I ran with, who had good or bad lymphoma. I pictured the nurse's brother lying in his hospital room, waiting for his sister to come to work the next morning, to sit by his bed and tell him about driving to Seattle to go running in the dark.

I'd like to say that I thought of Beth too. That I thought of her every moment that I trained for my race, the image of her in the MRI scanner bed or with a chemo-filled IV bag dangling above her motivating my every lap around the track or in the pool. But standing on the sidewalk three blocks from her old rental house whose living room I'd sat in too many times to count, I didn't think of her at all. As I walked around to unlock my car I scanned the sky, looking for the moon, but it was obscured by clouds or the apartment building across the street. I could not find it.

# 21. A Murder of Crows

One January afternoon I sat at my desk while Caleb napped, making a futile attempt to catch up on email, when Beth and Kevin knocked on the door. They'd just come from a visit to Beth's neuro-oncologist whose clinic sat less than two miles from our house.

"Look who's started bike training," Beth said, pointing to Kevin's bright yellow cycling jacket as they removed their shoes in the entryway.

"So I heard," I said. Kevin had sent an email the previous week, requesting donations for the Livestrong Foundation's charity event, held in Seattle for the first time that June. Kevin and a group of friends and family members had formed Team Bear, a tribute to Beth's childhood nickname.

"You've inspired him with your triathlon," Beth said. "I think you're both nuts." But she was smiling. Proud.

We went down to the basement, out of earshot of Caleb. I unfolded two spare dining chairs for Kevin and Beth, to protect her cat allergies. I sat on the couch and put Caleb's baby monitor on a side table.

"What are we listening to?' Beth asked, pointing to the monitor whose red lights lit and faded in time with music.

"A naptime CD I made him for Christmas," I said.

"A mix for the love of your life." She smiled. "So. How's the training going, champ?"

"How's the bike?" Kevin asked.

"In the shop," I said. "I had a little mishap."

"Did you crash?"

"I did," I said, and out came the story. Cycling was the most challenging of the three sports for me. A friend had told me about clipless pedals, which required special shoes. He advised getting them, to make my pedalling more efficient. The thought of mastering another aspect of cycling felt daunting, so I asked Matt to install toe clips instead. Coming to a stop on the bike trail a few weeks before, I forgot they were there. My foot still wedged into the clips, I tipped sideways, bike and body splatting onto the pavement. I got up quickly, as though the mistake could be undone if my bike and I were no longer prone on the trail. My rear wheel wouldn't spin. I was stuck. I flagged down a passing cyclist to help me attempt a roadside repair. He turned my bike upside-down so that the seat rested on the ground, the wheels in the air.

"Instant repair stand," he said as he peered at my rear wheel. He was a fire-fighter, he told me, on his way home from an overnight work shift. Two days before a man had walked onto the university campus, poured a can of gasoline over his head, and lit himself on fire. The firefighter's unit responded to the 911 call; he was on the relief shift. And now, on his way home from supporting his colleagues through the aftermath, he stopped to help me fix my bike.

After several minutes of attempted diagnoses, he figured out the problem.

"You bent your derailleur hangar," he told me, holding up a small, j-shaped piece of metal. Once flat, its stem now formed a hook.

"Your bike is broken," he said. "You can't ride it." We stood seven miles from my house. I fished my cell phone out of my pocket and called Matt.

"I'm worried," I said to Beth and Kevin after I finished

the story. "I think I might be the slowest cyclist in triathlon history." My Team in Training coach talked often about race time. She told us to estimate how long it would take us to do each segment and what our total time would be. I got anxious every time I tried to add it all up. Long, I thought to myself. Several hours.

I'd been obsessed with time since Caleb was born. There were feeding and sleep schedules to adhere to, which we'd only recently stopped tracking on a spiral notebook. Some days, time doled itself out in spoonfuls, inching towards the hour when Caleb would sleep and Matt and I could have a moment to ourselves. Mostly, though, the days dissolved into weeks, then months, like a time-lapse video of a flower blooming.

For Beth, I imagined, days passed more like a car with a faulty clutch. Sometimes she'd have energy for a walk on the beach with their dog or lunch with a friend. Other days fatigue would overwhelm her. Much of her time was taken up with the business of combating her cancer: consulting with naturopaths about disease-fighting foods, attending her brain tumour support group. She took her oral chemo pills on a schedule, removing them from her refrigerator and popping them through the foil backing, one by one. And always, the doctor's visits: scans, blood draws, long discussions, with and without her present, about how to keep her tumour at bay.

Finally, I asked Beth the question always on my mind.

"How are you feeling?" She looked out the window before answering, and my stomach clenched.

"The chemo isn't working," she said. "The tumour's getting bigger again." She would have to switch to IV chemo, meaning weekly visits to the clinic, for three hours at a stretch.

I watched her as she spoke. Tears formed in the corners of her eyes, then spilt out over reddened rims. Her cheeks immediately splotched, as though in an allergic reaction. I looked away from her face, at her magenta scarf that clashed with the canary walls. Matt and I had chosen the brightest colour we could stand for the basement, and made the fir-trimmed windows as large as possible. The blinds were turned horizontally to reveal spatters of rain like paint speckled Jackson Pollock-style on the pane behind Beth's head. This marked the fourteenth year of my friendship with Beth, and it was the first time I'd seen her cry. It would be the only time.

"I don't want to spend all that time at the clinic." she said as I reached behind me and handed her a box of tissues. "It makes me feel like even more of a cancer patient than I already am."

The oncology clinic was on the first floor of the hospital where she had her surgery. It was the same medical centre where I was treated for Crohn's, and I knew the drill: Park in the underground garage. Walk past the pay station, through the concrete-encased corridor with its birdsong recording piped through hidden speakers. I think it was meant to be soothing, but it was a lot of birds—several murders of crows, it seemed—chirping in an urgent tone. The effect always set my frayed nerves further on edge.

You rode the long escalator or waited for the elevator to shudder you up one level. It was cold in that corridor, damp and impersonal. The sky bridges from the parking lot at the children's hospital down the road were decorated with bright murals of whales and sea turtles, smiling octopi and wide-eyed clown fish. But what could they have painted the university medical centre corridor with to lessen the anxiety? No matter how calming the decorations, the facts remained the same: you were entering a building where you'd be poked, prodded, stripped naked, scanned, scoured. They used power tools on bones in that building, sharp scalpels to slice your flesh, staple guns to seal it shut. The items in their supply closets couldn't be that different, really, than those that filled the basements of serial killers.

*\*\*\**

In our basement, the baby monitor flashed red all the way to the end of the dial. Caleb, crying.

"He's awake," Beth said, blowing her nose once more. I gave her a look. "Let's go get him," she said before I could apologize for the timing. The three of us stood and ascended the stairs single-file, leaving the cat behind on the couch.

I changed Caleb's diaper and carried him into the living room. Kevin was sitting on the floor, cross-legged, and I plunked Caleb into his lap. I handed Kevin a board book and he began to read aloud. Beth followed me into the kitchen and talked to me while I unloaded the dishwasher.

"Don't worry about how slowly you cycle," she said. "You're going to ride your bike for twenty-five miles," she said, the number in italics as it emerged from her mouth. "Who cares what your time is?"

"You're right," I said, my false bravado obvious to us both.

Now, I want to go back to that January day and give myself a warning: Stop thinking about race time. Focus on Beth. The moment between now and when she dies will pass in an eye-blink.

She and Kevin gathered their belongings and said their goodbyes. After I closed the door behind them I lingered in the entryway, tucking shoes under the bench and hanging coats on hooks while behind me in the living room Caleb pulled books off the shelf one by one, arranging them into precarious stacks on the floor.

I watched out the window as Kevin opened the passenger door of their Subaru for Beth and helped her settle into her seat before going around to the driver's side. The fact that she would tolerate this act of chivalry indicated how sick she must have felt. She'd mastered a stick shift in that car; now she could barely get into it on her own. I stood by the front door, Caleb's rain boot in my hand, listening for the twin thuds of the car doors as they slammed shut against the afternoon's diminishing light.

# 22. The Call

Two weeks before the triathlon, as I leaned into our refrigerator, the phone rang. 5:00, the time people called our land line to ask us for money. It was my night to cook, and I was making my usual stand-by: pasta with red sauce and tofu dyed and shaped to look like ground beef. I shut the fridge door.

"Solicitor," I said to Matt as I walked into the living room, where he sat on the floor with Caleb. Late afternoons had become music time in our house, and the two of them fished around in an instrument-filled plastic bin for this evening's concert. Our phone's screen displayed the words private caller. Someone with a blocked number. I answered.

"Is Jane or Matt there?" said the voice on the other end of the line. Maybe it was a telemarketer after all. But I didn't mind. I was in a great mood, full of patience and good humour. That morning, I'd biked twenty miles, my last long ride before the race. When Matt got home from work he'd removed the pedals from my bike. The following morning I would drive downtown and deliver it to the Team in Training office for shipment. We would reunite, my bike and I, in Hawaii.

Matt, Caleb, and I were scheduled to leave Seattle a few days before the race. My Team in Training coach would spend two days familiarizing the team with the race course on the big island's south shore—the coral hazards in Anaehoʻomalu Bay, the potential gusts during the bike ride on Queen Kaahumanu Highway. We'd walk along a portion of the run course, which changed from lava rock to pavement to crushed shells, ending with a half-mile stretch on the sand.

While I spent time with the team, Matt and Caleb would enjoy the resort. To compensate for the lack of a swimming beach, the resort had constructed a series of elaborate pools. One had a waterfall and a corkscrew slide. One had a giant hot tub. One was a fake lagoon, with salt water and sand. The last pool was the resort's claim to fame: a place where, for a steep fee, hotel guests could swim with dolphins. I'd arranged for a diving company to take Matt out on a boat the day after the race, a small payback for the many hours of solo parenting he'd performed while I trained.

Lavaman drew a large contingent of Team in Training participants; over five hundred people from chapters across the country would be there to compete in the race. We'd have an "inspiration dinner" together the night before the race. They'd honour the top ten fundraisers, and present a prize to the person who'd raised the most money nationwide: Me.

I'd raised over $11,000, an astounding amount during the 2008 recession. It felt like Christmas every time I collected the mail. I got donations from uncles, friends, in-laws. A distant relative sent a check, so did a co-worker of Matt's I'd never met. The owner of a bed and breakfast Matt and I visited once two years before sent $100. The dentist Beth and I shared sent $250. They made me teary, these donations from near-strangers, and the ones from old friends too. A check came from an honorary aunt, the memo line filled in with the words *you go, girl*.

"You're getting a bike," our Team in Training chapter director told me. Not just any bike, she explained. On the stage in Hawaii, I'd be presented with a Trek racing bike with all of the trimmings—carbon-fibre frame and wheels, aero bars, eleven speeds. It would weigh less than Caleb. And I would be its owner. Me, who'd only recently learnt how to change a flat. An excited, nervous chill ran up my spine. I laughed.

"Really? Me?"

"Yes, you!" she said. "We are thrilled here at the office. Thank you so much for all of your efforts, Top Fundraiser." She giggled.

I'd raised money, and I'd trained. I rode my bike in the rain, went running in the snow and sleet. It was dark when I got up for Saturday morning team practices, and dark before I'd even turned on the stove to make dinner. I'd battled three colds during the training season, and nursed Caleb through his first stomach illness. Through everything, I'd had an image of myself crossing the finish line, its sponsor-labelled frame festooned with orchids and palm fronds. I'd pose for photos on the beach with Matt and Caleb, my finisher's medal around my neck, my cheeks flushed with a mixture of exertion, exhaustion, satisfaction. Victory.

*Is Jane there?* The caller said. Maybe it was not a solicitor. They usually called me by my last name, botching the pronunciation worse than acquaintances did. Who would be calling at that hour, the time of day when dinner preparation, arrival home from work, and toddler meltdown coalesce into a tempest of chaos? Who would call me Jane in an excited voice? Someone who didn't know me, but had news to deliver.

\*\*\*

During our first adoption wait, Matt and I took a trip to Hawaii's Big Island. We stayed at a bed and breakfast that didn't allow children under fourteen. We planned outings we wouldn't do if we had a baby in tow: a kayak trip to a snorkelling cove, a long drive to hike the steep trails of Volcanoes National Park. As with all of our other trips during our adoption wait, we sent our agency our itinerary so they could reach us if we got chosen while we were away.

Our second day there, we got a phone call, not from the agency, but from our next-door neighbour, who, along with her husband, had told us about the agency years before. The four of us completed our paperwork at the same time, and together, we waited.

"We got The Call," her voice cracked through my phone when I checked my messages after breakfast. "A baby boy, born yesterday." The next day I phoned her from a parking lot as Matt and I prepared to hike through a lava tube. She was at the hospital, changing the baby's diaper.

"People keep handing him to me and telling me he's my son," she said. "One of these times, I'll believe them." Later, on a narrow beach, Matt and I carved the baby's name and birth date into the black sand, photographing our work before the waves washed the letters away. I bought two Hawaiian-style outfits, one for the neighbours' baby, and a pair of tan and blue overall shorts for the baby we did not yet have. It was rare for me to buy myself baby gifts, rarer still for me to be so specific in my hope, to buy an outfit made for a boy who would be the right size to fit into it while the weather was warm.

Hawaii, then, had become more than just a vacation destination for me, or even a nice setting to do a triathlon. Before, it was a place I felt my childless state acutely. This time it would be a place I had the privilege of visiting with my son. We could take him to the beaches we'd strolled two years before, dreaming of him. We'd build castles and bury Daddy in the sand, then play in whatever gentle surf we could find.

***

"Is Jane there?" The caller said on the phone. I sat down at the dining room table, folding the unread newspaper that had been there since breakfast. I looked over at Caleb, shaking a tiny tambourine while he sat on the living room floor. He'd long since outgrown his Hawaii outfit, getting to wear it only once for his first birthday party before it got too small.

"This is Jan-et," I said into the phone.

"Oh, I'm sorry," the caller laughed. "I knew that. It actually says Janet on the paper in front of me. This is Jodi. I'm an adoption counsellor." As she said the name of our adoption agency, my heart thudded in a way it had only once before, with the phone call for Caleb two years before.

It wasn't that I'd forgotten that we'd been waiting to adopt a baby. Not exactly. But I'd been so busy with Caleb, with training for Lavaman, that I didn't have time to think about the wait, an event that had been my whole world the first time around.

"Hi, Jodi," I said, over-bright and way too loud, the way I imagine I would if Ed McMahon showed up on my porch with a check the size of the dining room table where I sat. I turned to look at Matt, behind me with Caleb on the living room floor. I bugged my eyes, mouthing the name of our agency. Matt's faced turned cartoon, eyes saucered, lips curled in a tidy circle.

"I'm calling to tell you that you've been picked by an expectant parent," Jodi said. I didn't have time to register this with more than one high-jump-sized heart beat before the next sentence came.

"She has a baby girl due soon. Really soon, actually. March 22nd."

Years later, I would still feel shame at my heart's next movement: a drop downward onto the high jump mat, the bar knocked to the ground. I knew exactly how soon March 22nd would come. The date had already been stamped two places: the front of my brain, and the top of our plane tickets to Hawaii.

# 23. Helen

We met our daughter's birth parents, Mark and Terri, at the food court of the mall near their house. Matt and I spotted the Subway counter where we'd planned to meet, then saw Terri at a table in front, beaming and waving. She stood up to shake our hands. She was nearly six feet, and her centre-parted red curls fell halfway down her back. Gold-rimmed glasses obscured her wide-set blue eyes. I memorized the details of her face, and Mark's when he walked up to our table a few minutes later: his shapely-tipped nose and long, dark lashes.

It felt crass, this assessment of their features less like the behaviour of a prospective adoptive parent, more like that of a horse trader. I'm not sure it's possible, though, to meet your future child's birth parents and not give them a thorough looking-over for signs of genetic defects or pathological aspects to their personality you might be able to detect in their eyes. But they looked fine, good even. The four of us stood there, smiling shyly at one another.

"I recognized you from your photos," Terri said and gave a small laugh. Most of her sentences were punctuated by this little laugh, a characteristic I liked immediately. Jodi, the agency counsellor, arrived and we began our official meeting.

Mark and Terri lived together, Jodi had told us over the phone. He wanted to get married. She didn't. Mark wanted to raise the baby; Terri already had her hands full parenting two teenagers.

"Mark is coming around to the idea of adoption," Jodi had said. Indeed, he seemed to warm to the concept over the course of the meeting, brightening when we told him we met up with Caleb's birthmom and her son every few months, at a halfway point between our homes.

Meeting your unborn child's birth parents and discussing an adoption agreement in a food court felt about as surreal as it sounds. Toddlers screeched, teenagers howled with laughter, wives and husbands bickered, employees called out food orders around us while we talked. It was a very public place to have such an intimate conversation, but no one around us noticed or cared.

"What about names?" Jodi said.

"Helen for the first name," I said. Matt and I had made the decision years before. We each had a grandmom named Helen, and had chosen that as our daughter's name long before our marriage, the pregnancy attempts, the adoption plans.

"We were hoping you'd help us choose the middle name," Matt said. We listed a few we'd considered.

"Alexandra?" I said. Terri brightened. Alexander was her oldest son's middle name. I explained Caleb's middle name symmetry with his birth family's last name.

"Helen Alexandra," Jodi said, smiling. "I love it. Very Greek."

***

The obstetrician's name vanished from my memory the moment after he told it to me. It was mid-day a week after our food court meeting, and we'd all come to the hospital on the doctor's schedule: Matt and me, Terri and Mark. Terri was one of three women he induced that morning, deliveries he wanted to preside over before he left for Arizona the next morning.

"A conference in Phoenix," he told Matt and me. "And golfing." He smiled with a mouth that looked like it was made of wax. "I want to deliver the baby myself, since I took care of Mom during her pregnancy." I wondered if he called Terri "Mom" because he couldn't remember her name. I wondered what Terri thought of his caretaking skills. I wondered a lot of things about Terri and Mark, whom Matt and I had spent a total of two hours with before joining them in the delivery room.

At the hospital, the baby seemed in no hurry to emerge. At 5:00 p.m. Terri's cervix remained dilated at two centimetres, where it had been all afternoon. Mark had left to work the evening shift at Safeway an hour before, leaving Matt and I alone with Terri and the hospital staff.

Terri reclined in bed in a hospital gown, her hair in a loose ponytail, the sheet pulled up to her waist. A wide elastic band encircled her abdomen, its monitor hooked up to a different display. We could hear the slow beep of Helen's heartbeat.

"How about sitting on the ball?" the nurse said.

"I'm more comfortable lying down," Terri said.

They had this conversation every thirty minutes or so, the nurse telling Terri her cervix would dilate to a ten—the number at which she could start pushing—more quickly if she sat on the large, inflated ball beside the bed. Terri smiled and ignored her advice.

Though I felt impatient for the delivery, I admired Terri's defiance. During my hospitalizations, I always did whatever the doctors and nurses told me to do. But this was Terri's fourth baby. She was the expert on the way her body behaved while in labour, not some nurse she'd met only hours before. What were Terri's other deliveries like? Was she thinking now of her other daughter, whom she'd placed for adoption ten years before, and never heard from since? I didn't feel I knew Terri well enough to ask her. I didn't feel Matt and I knew her well enough to be here now, at this private moment, supporting her through an experience we'd never had ourselves.

Terri asked for us to come, I reminded myself. The adoption counsellor presented her with different options, and she'd said she wanted us there in the room.

So we made small talk. When we ran out of conversation topics, we turned on the television. No one acknowledged the mix of emotions, the joy and fear and loss churning together in the over-crowded, too-hot room. From time to time, Terri said "I'm tired," with a wide smile on her face. Never: It hurts. This is hard. This isn't how this was supposed to go.

I looked out the window. A playground sat on the other side of the fence from the hospital, the grass worn down to dirt under the swings. I thought of Caleb. My mom had flown in the day before to take care of him, and I wondered what they'd done all afternoon. Gone to the playground, maybe, where Caleb no doubt bypassed the swings and sat in the sand, playing with a broken dump truck or cement mixer someone had abandoned there. He'd wear the down coat he inherited from his cousin and the orange wool hat Matt's brother gave him for Christmas, its brim shadowing his wind-reddened cheeks.

***

At 11:00 p.m. I looked over at Terri, sitting on the ball at last. Her hair had come out of its ponytail holder and hung in curtains on either side of her face. She looked exhausted, like she'd already delivered the baby. Maybe if we weren't in the room, these virtual strangers who were going to take her baby home, she'd be more at ease. Maybe Matt's and my presence was delaying the delivery. I stood up.

"Matt and I are going to go lie down in the lobby," I said, making the decision for both of us.

"Good idea," said the nurse. "I'll come get you if any-thing happens." On the couch, I fell asleep immediately.

An hour later, the nurse shook my shoulder.

"Terri's getting an epidural," she said. "She can have one person sit with her. She asked for you." I followed her down the hall, leaving Matt sleeping on the couch behind me. I rubbed my face, felt a crease on my left cheek where it had pressed too long against the couch cushion. One per-son, and she'd asked for me. Maybe I didn't make her un-easy after all. Maybe that's why she'd chosen Matt and me as adoptive parents. Maybe, like Caleb's birthmom Bree, she felt a sense of familiarity when she first saw our photo. Comfort. Trust.

In the room, I held the wheeled table in place while Terri gripped its side, her legs dangling off the edge of the bed. The anaesthesiologist inserted the needle at the base of her spine, giving directions in a bored voice. After he finished he packed his cart up wordlessly. Red-faced, he left the room with a muttered goodbye. The door closed, and the three of us laughed.

"I think women make him nervous," the nurse said. "Or at least ones about to deliver a baby." Terri leaned back in bed, closed her eyes, and pushed her breath out all at once.

"Almost time," the nurse said.

And then it was. I went to wake Matt and we jogged back to the room. Two nurses helped Terri place her feet in the stirrups.

"Stand here," one nurse said, positioning Matt by Terri's shoulders and me by her left foot.

The doctor came in and washed his hands. He sat down on a wheeled stool and held his balled-up paper towel aloft.

"Bank off the left side," he said, a basketball player predicting his shot into the trash can. He missed.

"Oh, good try," the nurse said, playing along. I looked at Matt and he shrugged his shoulders. The doctor tipped a plastic shield in front of his face and turned to Terri.

"Push," he said, and counted down from ten in an overloud voice, even though Terri wasn't making any noise herself. She was the quietest person in the room, her cheeks ripened tomatoes, her red curls spilling over her shoulders.

"You had the Dad View," a friend observed when I described being in the delivery room for Caleb's birth. I had the Dad View right then, standing between the doctor and Terri's right leg. Cutting the cord is the bone doctors throw to fathers, I decided, a way to make them feel more involved in the birth. Only, I didn't want to be the Dad. I wanted to be the Mom. I wasn't the one who carried and delivered the baby. I wouldn't be breastfeeding. But I could be the Mom in every other way, like with Caleb, plus some girl-y touches: taking my daughter out for tea and watching her ballet recitals.

My daughter.

"This is Helen," I would say to Caleb the next morning at home when, still in his jungle-themed pyjamas, he met her for the first time. "Your sister."

The head emerged. Seconds later, the final push ended in a splatter of blood and amniotic fluid on the floor. Helen came out yelling, just like Caleb did, no doctor-slap needed, her tiny lungs pushing out sound, sucking in breath, rapid-fire, her heartbeat fast as a hummingbird's, and mine staccatoed too, the sound of her cry thrumming against my eardrums, my ribcage, the roots of my hair.

"Who's cutting the cord?" the doctor asked. I turned to Matt, standing at Terri's shoulder, out of direct view of the most private part of her. We hadn't discussed ahead of time who would perform this act, our one delivery room role. How had we forgotten?

"Do you want to do it?" I said. The Dad cuts the cord.

"You should do it," he said. "I already got to." Would this divide our family along gender lines, Matt cutting our son's cord, me cutting our daughter's? Would it bond Helen to me the way that Caleb was attached to Matt, more deeply and innately, it seemed, than he was connected to me? There wasn't time to think about it. The doctor handed me the scissors.

I made the cut.

# 21. Down in the Hole

"Sounds like reflux," our paediatrician said when I described Helen's behaviour at her two-week checkup. She spat up with every feeding, and often writhed in pain. She emitted a constant screech more characteristic of an avian newborn than a human one. She couldn't lie on her back to sleep without vomiting, so she slept in her swing at night, and attached to me or Matt with one of our three baby-wearing apparatuses during the day.

Our bedroom felt crowded, Helen's empty crib wedged between our bed and the wall, the swing she slept in alongside the rocking chair. We stored her clothes in Caleb's dresser, pulling out small stacks of pyjamas each evening before he went to sleep in case she required a middle-of-the-night outfit change. We created a makeshift changing station on the floor next to the swing, and a large dresser filled the remaining wall. It felt like sleeping in a storage room full of rotten milk. I longed for time to re-organize our house.

Not enough time seemed to be Matt's and my slogan, ever since we'd brought Helen home. A few weeks before the counsellor called, I bought several skeins of yarn to make a blanket for the birthmom of our second child, just as I'd done the first time around. When would I ever have time to do that now?

Even though we'd made plans to visit Mark and Terri a month after Helen's birth, even though no one had cried at our parting in the hospital lobby, I'd been unable to entirely shake the sad feeling from the hospital room. Something felt off once we returned home, the opposite of how I'd felt the first time around. From the very beginning, Caleb felt like my son, the child I was meant to parent. He was born at the summer solstice, and we spent long, lazy days lounging on blankets in the park, taking leisurely walks in our neighbourhood in the evenings. Matt and I read to him every evening before bed, and, in my recollection, spent a lot of time smiling, tickling, cooing. We were exhausted, sure, and our lives were upended, but in ways which we had hoped for and anticipated.

Helen, in contrast, arrived abruptly into our full and busy lives. Her birth caused a disruption, a need to reconfigure our routine, but when, and how? Trying to parent an infant and a toddler at the same time made me feel as unnatural at caretaking as I'd been when I started babysitting at age twelve, like if you didn't give me specific instructions, I might accidentally feed Helen diaper cream.

\*\*\*

"I think we should start a new TV show, to help us get through the feedings," I said to Matt one morning as we looked at each other, bleary-eyed, across the breakfast table. Bottle feeding was a shared duty. We alternated nights, with one parent doing the 10 p.m. feeding, the other taking the 2 a.m. shift. 10 p.m. was the most challenging, Matt and I craving sleep, Helen's digestive pain at its worst.

During Caleb's infancy, feedings took twelve minutes. I read novels while I fed him, one hand on the bottle, the other on the book. Helen's reflux required an elaborate procedure of feed, burp, clean vomit, repeat. She had to be held upright for fifteen minutes after the feeding ended. The entire process took an hour or more, and required both hands. The only books I'd opened in months were the children's stories I read to Caleb at bedtime.

"TV would probably help," Matt said.

"How about The Wire?"

"Isn't that really violent and depressing?"

"It's violent. I don't know about depressing. Everyone says it's really well-written." Matt shrugged in assent, and I placed the Netflix order. By the end of the second episode, we were both hooked. The 10 p.m. feeding became the shift we looked forward to, settling on the couch with Helen, the remote resting on the couch arm.

I spent hours in the same position on that couch, as many, I would wager, as I did while recovering from surgery. If Caleb was awake during Helen's feeding, we selected from our box set of Scholastic DVDs; Caleb sat next to Helen and me on the couch while cartoon images from *Make Way for Ducklings* or *Chicka Chicka Boom Boom* flickered across the screen. At night, while Caleb slept in his crib in the next room, The Wire imparted its potluck of family values. We watched a newly imprisoned Wee-Bay pass his drug-dealing business onto his son. McNulty, the alcoholic, philandering detective enlisted his young sons in a game of "front and follow" when he spotted arch-villain Stringer Bell in the grocery store. I'm guessing that when Richard Price, a contributing writer on the show, wrote the scene where Detective Greggs and her three-year-old son say a *Goodnight Moon*-style farewell to the dealers and addicts below their apartment window, he did not have actual child viewers in mind.

While the evenings were hard, daytime, when both kids were awake, was the most difficult. Caring for Helen re-

quired patience, the slow feedings, the changing of diaper after diaper. Caleb, at a year and a half, was like a bug
trapped in an inverted jar, buzzing from one end of the
house to the other, his engine set to full throttle as long as
he was conscious.

It felt some kind of martial arts test or Buddhist ritual,
the way I should have been able to cleave myself. Or maybe I needed to think of myself as bionic, my right hand
moving slowly over Helen's body, my right darting out to
grab Caleb as he zipped past. When Matt was home, we
played one-on-one defence, one of us chasing our pinball
son around the house, while the other cared for our alter-
nately shrieking, milk-spewing daughter. Someone walking
by our house in the evenings might have thought we were
being burglarized or murdered.

Before Caleb was born, we'd attended a talk about post-
partum depression sponsored by our adoption agency.

"Anyone can experience it," the psychologist told the
group. "Biological parents, adoptive parents, mothers, fathers, grandparents who are primary caregivers."

Did I have it? Was I simply tired? The abrupt reversal of
my fitness level couldn't have helped, nor the hours I spent
watching a show whose characters spent so much time, as
Tom Waits intoned in the theme song, "way down in the
hole."

And then there was the fact that Beth was dying, something we simultaneously knew and didn't know. She still
had seizures too often to drive, and a month before Helen
was born we'd talked of reviving our Driving Miss Peterman ritual. After we brought Helen home, though, Beth
and I never spoke of it again. I assumed she'd found someone with a car free of screeching infants to take her, someone who could reliably arrive at her house on time, well-
rested, and freshly showered.

I longed for time alone with Beth, or at least time together without the kids. But that opportunity did not exist.
The hours swam together: night, day, toddler, newborn,
changing diapers, bathing, buckling into high chairs, car
seats, swings. *Not enough time. Not enough time.*

# 25. Attitude is Everything

And then there was the day I made the babysitter cry.

I sat on my deck in the faint April sun. The babysitter put Caleb down for a nap, then sat down on the opposite side of the dimpled glass table. We could hear Caleb on the baby monitor performing his humming-rocking-head-banging routine in the crib, his lullaby music playing in the background. Matt and I owned a set of CDs featuring rock music played on soothing marimbas. I couldn't tell which album was playing, Caleb mostly drowned it out, but I guessed it was Nirvana. That was the babysitter's favourite.

One-month-old Helen had just fallen asleep in the sling in my lap, and I rocked gently in the chair as I talked. She needed constant movement during sleep, and I needed her to stay asleep. Desperately.

I gave a modified version of a speech I recited to the babysitter two months before, pre-Helen. Back then, I used a gentle tone, politely suggesting that she spend less time in coffee shops with Caleb and more time doing, well, anything else. I reminded her about the children's museum and zoo memberships I had bought for her, the list of indoor activities I had researched and compiled.

"If all else fails you can take the bus somewhere. Caleb loves riding the bus," I'd said with a smile.

This time, though, I was pissed, and too tired to conceal

it.

The babysitter was only in charge of Caleb, and I saw her job as similar to that of a dog-sitter: run him hard all morning, feed him occasionally, and put him down for a nap. She'd worked for us for over a year, and she and Caleb had previously enjoyed a varied and satisfying routine. More and more frequently, though, their entire morning was spent at one of several cafés with play spaces. I could imagine the scene: the babysitter sitting at a table, drinking coffee and talking on her cell phone. Caleb, elbowing for space at the train table, driving a broken dump truck across a carpet littered with Annie's Organic Cheddar Bunny Cracker crumbs.

Out on the deck, I laid out my unhappiness with their daily itinerary. I highlighted the need for more physical activity, for more emotional and intellectual stimulation. She played the role of errant pupil, and I, the principal, complete with stern lecture delivered in an impatient tone. And then I made the mistake of issuing a psychological evaluation.

"It seems like you're burnt out on the job."

"No, I'm not," she said, and began to cry. Normally, I would experience a surge of guilt at reducing someone to tears. But mostly what I felt was a spreading coldness, born from an exhaustion I thought might never dissipate.

"I'm just tired," she said after a minute of crying. I suppressed a laugh, that's how cruel my mood was. Apparently sleep-deprivation drained my sympathy gland. I couldn't summon the strength to feel sorry for the babysitter, because that would take energy away from feeling sorry for myself. Did anyone have a more stressful existence than me at that very moment?

***

Well, of course, there was Beth.

One morning she and Kevin stopped by the house on their way to the doctor's office to get the results of her latest MRI. Beth seemed keyed up, as I imagine she often was before those appointments. The doctor would enter the room with his thumb up or down, she told me, and then they'd make a plan.

"Hello, beautiful," she said to Helen, settling into the leather chair and holding her arms out. I transferred Helen from my lap to hers and draped a dish towel over Beth's shoulder.

"She hasn't eaten in awhile," I told Beth. "But it's best to take universal precautions."

I don't remember what Beth wore that day. A turtleneck sweater, let's say, because it was early April and she was perpetually cold. The teal one. And khaki pants, tapered at her ankles. Her hair, which she'd shaved pre-surgery eight months before, had grown into a stylish, cropped hairdo. We talked about Ted Kennedy's health insurance bill.

"Dying of brain cancer, and look at how hard he's working," Beth said.

"Aren't you working?" I said.

"Yeah, but just a few hours a week from home. I need to in order to keep my health insurance." A little laugh of resignation escaped from her throat.

"What? That's bullshit." I'd been in the same position when I did my library internship the fall of my first surgery. But this was worse. She had brain cancer. She worked for the foundation's global health team. Couldn't they bring the same compassion that guided their international work to the health care of their own employees?

"It is, but what can I do?" Beth said. She paused. "If Kennedy's bill passes, it will be a miracle."

I wish I could say that Beth's last visit to my house lasted all day, that she and Kevin stayed for dinner, that we talked about the meaning of life while the sun set and the moon rose. That Mary Poppins arrived at the door to take care of Caleb and Helen for the evening. That during dessert, Beth's tumour dissolved into little crumbs that she combed out of her hair and rinsed down the bathtub drain.

After less than an hour at my house, though, she went to her doctor's appointment. We had to interrupt ourselves, as usual, before we were finished talking. We said goodbye at the door and exchanged an awkward hug, me balancing Helen in the crook of one arm, Beth with her right-sided numbness. Two working arms between us.

\*\*\*

Two days later I settled on my couch with Helen asleep on my lap. Matt and Caleb were at the playground. It was one of those warm spring days when the sun beamed down on our rain-slicked neighbourhood. Everything bloomed and the smell of cherry blossoms, lilacs, daphnia on our corner filled even cranky, sleep-deprived moms with a childlike delight.

Matt had left our front door cracked open to allow some fresh air to seep into our fetid living room. I felt ready for a marathon phone chat. There was only one voice I wanted to hear on the other end of the line. I dialled Beth's number.

"How are you?" I asked when she picked up. "What happened at the doctor's?"

"Chemo fail number four." The cancer caused her words

to emerge in a slow, tipsy-sounding slur. The medicine was supposed to slow the tumour's growth. Instead, the cancer had begun to spider itself through the contours of her brain. Her doctors sent her chart to a research hospital in California to see if she could qualify for a clinical trial. The same hospital had seen her records six years before, for the first tumour. Normally, they required an in-person visit for such a consultation, but back then she'd skirted the regulations because her supervisor at the foundation had a personal connection to one of the doctors.

"I'm hoping I can pretend I've already been down there," she said, with a laugh and a muffled sniffle over the phone line. "It's a lie, but only a small one." At the sound of Beth crying, tears started in my own eyes. I forced a laugh out too, my mind tripping over itself as I searched it for the right thing to say—something clever, yet supportive. In truth, I felt horrified to think of Beth participating in a clinical trial. That seemed like a last-resort action. Beth wasn't at that stage. Was she?

"I have to go," Beth said, filling the silence I'd created while I urged the sleep-gummed motor in my brain to turn over. "Sorry I can't talk longer. We're on our way out of town for the weekend. I'll call you next week." It's rare that you know in advance the last words someone will say to you, or you to them. Rare that you get a chance to find the profound thing, the perfect thing to say. We would talk next week. Beth believed this, and so did I.

"Okay," I said. "Take care. Talk to you soon." I hung up. I looked down at Helen, then around the room. The colour seemed to have drained from everything in the two minutes since I'd picked up the phone. It felt like the moment when the sun goes behind a cloud, though the actual sunshine still streamed through the windows, forming rectangles of light across the floor.

A gust of wind sucked the door shut with a slam. Helen started awake and began crying. I sprung to my feet and, began dipping and swaying, a return-to-sleep dance step Matt and I learnt during Caleb's infancy. As I bent and straightened my legs, I put my mouth close to Helen's ear, telling her over and over, it's okay, it's okay, it's okay. I bounced up and down until she stopped crying, and then kept bouncing slowly, stroking the layer of fuzz covering the soft spot on her skull.

***

All over town, friends and family exercised on Beth's behalf, preparing for the Livestrong Challenge in late June. I learnt of another Team in Training triathlon that would take place in California in the fall.

"Really?" Matt said when I told him I wanted to sign up. "You want to start training again now? So soon?" I watched as he scanned the living room scattered with toys, burp cloths, the detritus of our child-rearing.

"I already have all of the money raised," I said. "I'm still mostly in shape from Lavaman training. Plus, Beth." I trailed off. Matt stopped scanning, looked me in the eye and nodded. He understood the real reason, the one I couldn't say aloud: I wanted to do the race before Beth died.

As with our adoptions, I pretended that cancer had a predictable timeline. Surely this was how the disease always operated: Beth would be informed of how much time she had left, told to get her affairs in order. Then she'd call each of her friends and family to dispense the last of her old-soul wisdom. We'd brew a special batch of beer, make pasta and pie crust from scratch, and throw Beth the mother of all parties. Sleater-Kinney would play. Sherman Alexie would recite a poem he'd written for her. We'd fly Ted Kennedy in to present her with the health care bill he'd helped pass into law, expedited in Beth's honour.

\*\*\*

Trying to focus on events within my control, I considered firing the babysitter. I visited preschools, signed up for waiting lists. I went to the grocery store, the paediatrician's office. At home, Matt and I attended to the business of parenting: feeding, diapers, laundry, dishes. We slept in fragments, and showered infrequently. Everything gathered in unattended piles like stacks of newspapers in a hoarder's house: bills, architectural drawings, hand-me-down clothes for Helen sent by friends. We'd be moving into a rental house around the corner in July so our remodel could begin. I did not know how we could get all of our things packed in time. I'd once been an organized person, someone who wrote thank-you notes and kept a tidy filing system in my home office. That spring, phone calls went unanswered, emails piled in my inbox, waiting me for take action.

On my birthday Beth emailed me a card. Her message scrolled across the screen as a fairy decorated a cake, lit and blew out candles: *So glad your bundle of joy arrived in time for your birthday!* She left a birthday greeting on my voicemail that I listened to once before deleting. I emailed a few times, then stopped when I didn't hear back, just as I'd done during our eight-month rift. I called and listened to the phone ring with that same sick feeling, waiting for the voice mail to pick up.

Beth started a blog to keep on top of communication

with friends and family. She called it *Off the Top of My Head*, the title she'd chosen for her memoir, one of a half-dozen projects schemed to document her life. Another was a book we planned write together. We would alternate chapters, discussing her brain tumours, my butt tumours, and the antics of being a patient. It would be brilliant: sarcastic, and poignant, a decisive skewering of the medical establishment.

"What does it say about our places in the universe," I said once, "that your tumour was in your brain and mine was in my butt?"

"What does it say," Beth said, "that yours was benign and mine was malignant?"

*Life is beautiful*, Beth wrote on her blog. When I read those words I thought, *oh shit*. She wasn't prone to sunny platitudes, but her cynicism always went dormant when she got sick.

An image of Beth lying in the bed of the MRI scanner or on her couch at home napping more frequently than Helen would float into my consciousness and I would want to reach for the phone. By the time I had a spare half-second to do so, though, I would have forgotten my intention. Instead, Beth's health hovered near the surface of my brain, like a half-remembered song from childhood, the lyrics trying to make their way through the fog of memory to the tip of my tongue.

"Bring me your stories," Beth said on her blog, inviting friends to her house. The only stories I possessed involved Helen's shit or vomit, one or both of which was usually in evidence on my clothes during the telling. But Beth wouldn't have cared. It would have been so easy to call her, to offer to bring her lunch, to stop by for a short visit. I could have arrived on her doorstep with both kids in tow, all of us unwashed, none able to speak in full sentences, including me. She would have greeted us with a smile, brought out the toy box they kept for visitors.

***

May arrived, and with it a letter from preschool: Caleb was in for the fall. I felt alarmed by how happy this made me, my son's first acceptance letter. I offered the babysitter a summer schedule I knew she would not agree to, and together we chose her last day of employment. It was a passive-aggressive firing, the most I could do with the emotional energy I was able muster.

I awoke one morning to see a note on the blog, saying Beth had just boarded an aeroplane headed to Europe. She went against her doctor's advice, Kevin would tell me later. I imagined her deliberation: Should she go? What would happen if her condition worsened while she was away? Maybe she looked up the French phrase for brain tumour. Maybe she used the meditation tape I gave her, followed the instructions to visualize herself healthy and strong.

Back at the computer, I wondered why Beth hadn't called me before she left. I felt a wobble of insecurity as I speculated the reasons for her silence: anger at me, or indifference. I did not understand that her reasons for not calling or visiting were the same as mine. We did not possess the strength to help each other; we could barely help ourselves. Our positions of giving and receiving care had always been traded off. We weren't capable of playing both roles simultaneously.

It sounds ludicrous in hindsight: I felt jealous of Beth for being able to take a spontaneous vacation. Envious of the friends who went with her, for getting time with Beth that

I wanted for myself. I felt guilty for these thoughts, and worse when I wondered if the daughter I waited so long for arrived at exactly the wrong time. I did not realize that I would need her desperately to survive what was about to come.

Someone posted photos online from the trip, a travelogue detailing bucolic surroundings and delectable meals. I should have focused on Beth's grin as she partook of a cheese plate the size of Nebraska. Instead, I could not ignore her lopsided smile. Her cheeks were puffed from steroid medication. Goddamn Prednisone, I thought as I looked at the images.

I imagine that she sensed that death was near. What did it feel like to carry that knowledge within her, so far from home? To touch Italian soil for the first and last time, to lie in bed at night listening to the water clack against the boats in the harbor below? Was every action, every sensory experience, laden with meaning as they developed into a series of last times? If I'd been with her in Europe, I might've asked Beth those questions, appropriate or not. And when she looked me in the eye and answered honestly, as she always did, I would not have known what to say.

\*\*\*

Beth returned from Europe on a Sunday. She had a chemo treatment the following Tuesday. Glued to my desk chair, I read Kevin's emails about her deteriorating condition. Over the course of three days, she became unable to move her entire right side. The pauses between words lengthened, as though the ink printed on the dictionary in her brain began to fade. Despite this, invitations were extended for all to come and see Beth at the Livestrong event the upcoming weekend. She would be at the sidelines to cheer everyone on: her family, her friends, the countless cancer survivors who proudly collected their yellow roses at the finish line. Someone would get a rose for Beth. Maybe Kevin would ride across the line with the stem between his teeth, dismount from his bike and walk on rubbery legs to place it at her feet.

On Thursday, Caleb turned two. My parents flew into town to help us celebrate. I sent Beth an email asking if Matt and I could come over while my parents babysat. I ended with that vague offer, *let me know if there's anything I can do to help*. I didn't understand that Beth could no longer check her email, or answer the phone. Everything fell to Kevin— communication with doctors, with family and friends. He was having to take over the role of decision-maker and caregiver, making hard choices for them both: should she go to the hospital, or have hospice come to their house? Do the Livestrong ride as planned or stay at her bedside? Friends came over to help Kevin build a wheelchair ramp off the back of the house. She never used it.

\*\*\*

Our house was a clutter of half-packed boxes, so we held Caleb's party in the backyard of our rental. Matt and I helped Caleb blow out the candles on his blueberry-topped vanilla cake. I took a photograph of Caleb and a neighbour sitting on the floor of the empty living room. Tucked in an album in some box, back at our house, another photo, another empty living room: Beth and Kevin and Matt in our newly purchased home. Beers at their feet, their bodies spread-eagled to indicate vastness.

Then Sunday came, and with it, the Livestrong Challenge. Our family arrived at a strange in-between stage: the five kilometre run long over, the bike ride still in progress. Discarded water bottles and PowerBar wrappers littered the grass. "Clocks" by Coldplay blasted through the loudspeaker, Chris Martin singing about lights going out and not being able to be saved. Banners decorated the finish line chute, emblazoned with the Livestrong motto: Unity is Strength. Knowledge is Power. Attitude is Everything.

People wandered across the large lawn adjacent to the finish, stopping to buy sweatshirts and baseball caps at the vendor booths. Children squealed as they played in the fountain in the centre of the square, and rode down a giant inflatable slide placed at one end of the quadrangle for the duration of the event. Everyone strolled, unhurried, as though they were at a town picnic instead of an athletic event.

I looked across the crowd, searching the spectators for a shock of red hair. I envisioned Beth sitting in the grass at the sidelines, her tan baseball cap shielding her pale face from the sun. I felt anxious to sit beside Beth, to watch her tickle Helen under her double chin. We'd laugh as Beth told stories of driving through the French countryside. I'd tell her about the rocket ship-shaped foam wedge the paediatrician had given us for Helen, allowing her sleeping spot to shift, finally, to from her swing to her crib. We would marvel that we'd gone so long—over two months—without seeing each other. As with our eight month gap in communication from years ago, we wouldn't wonder aloud why it had happened. We'd just move on.

"Can Helen and I bring you lunch on Tuesday?" I'd say.

"Only if you bring chocolate too," she'd reply.

But Beth wasn't there. Walking up and down the quad, I didn't see anyone I knew. Had we missed the riders? I called her cousin, the logistical coordinator for the day.

I can pinpoint the exact moment when the bottom fell out of my world. Not when I visited Beth's bedside two days later, holding her hand as she lay in a morphine-induced sleep. Not when Kevin called the following morning to tell me she was gone. The free-fall began as I stood on one edge of the wide expanse of lawn, the finish line to my right, cell phone mashed into my ear, the blare of music muffling her cousin's words.

"Beth's not going to make it today," he said, meaning she wasn't coming to the race. But I heard the statement as though he were a psychic or a doctor making a pronouncement. *Beth's not going to make it.*

# 26. A Fissure in the Sky

The day before Beth died I sat at the foot of the hospital bed in the front room of her house, watching her sleep while I tried to think of something to say. Sun shot through a cloudless sky, spilling light onto the honey wood floor and her copper hair splayed across the pillow. Matt sat next to me, a sleeping Helen in his lap, a drawing Caleb had made that morning on the blanket between us. We'd left Caleb and the new babysitter back at home, making play dough.

Beth's arms formed two vertical lines on top of the sheets tucked neatly under her armpits. Someone folded those sheets, maybe one of the people assembled in the living room when we arrived—Kevin, Beth's aunt, her brother. Her friend Khampo, clad in an apron, stood in the kitchen sautéing vegetables. Kevin's family, who'd travelled from Sitka for the Livestrong ride, cancelled their return tickets and remained in town, waiting.

Beth slept sitting up. She wore a blue t-shirt I did not recognize. I thought she'd be cold in short sleeves, but when I picked up her hand, it felt warm. She looked different than she had the last time I'd seen her two months before. Her hair, shaved nearly a year ago for surgery, had grown out to bob-length, just below her ears. The steroid medication puffed her cheeks slightly, not nearly to the degree of my own Prednisone-induced inflation. Her skin appeared as pale as always, with a scattering of freckles under her eyes.

She breathed deeply, evenly, like Helen when she slept.

A hospital-issue toilet sat against one wall; a bedside table held a red velvet ribbon-wrapped candle and a glass of water with a straw. A copy of David Sedaris' *Holidays on Ice* lay on a futon by the window. Beth's nephew had bought a zebra mask for her; it sat on the bed above her left shoulder, keeping watch.

"Remember my amoebic dysentery in Ecuador?" I said finally. "The lab tech ate a popsicle while she analyzed my sample." I told her how we wondered if the popsicle itself had gotten sick as if she hadn't been there, as if she wasn't the one who made the joke. In Ecuador, we'd doubled over with laughter. By Beth's bed, I forced a smile while she slept, unresponsive.

"Don't go yet," I wanted to say. I'm not ready. I thought I was supposed to tell her we would be alright, that it was okay to go. But I was in a panic. How were we going to be able to go on without her?

"I'm sorry I didn't come sooner," I should have said. "I'm here now. Wake up and talk to me. Tell me you'll pull out of it. Tell me you'll be okay. Tell me what to do."

\*\*\*

In the evening, as Beth's breaths slowed and her family gathered around her bed, I stood in my entryway across town, buckling Helen into our jogging stroller. In the kitchen, Matt washed dinner dishes and baby bottles. Caleb was already asleep, the stuffed bear Beth gave him when he was three days old lying face up at the foot of his crib. Half-filled boxes lined the walls of every room. Somehow, we would finish packing in time to move the following week.

I ran down the hill to a trail by the lake. Helen fell asleep within minutes, and I detoured off the path to a park, pushing the stroller in front of me. I stopped at the edge of the lake by a stand of blackberry bushes whose fruit had not yet ripened. I watched the weekly sailing race, boats zipping around buoys in front of the downtown skyline. At the restaurant adjacent to the park, diners clinked glasses and forked locally caught salmon under plum-coloured umbrellas. The sun, three days past the summer solstice, shone on the water and the tops of trees.

A sailboat approached the drawbridge to my left, honking its horn to request passage. The bridge operator responded with five short blasts of his own. The boat idled in front of me, waiting. When traffic cleared, the bridge would rise, allowing space for the boat to pass.

I watched the boaters sip beers twenty feet from me, laughing, none of us aware that early the next morning, at the moment the sun created a fissure in the night sky, Beth would breathe her final breath.

The bell above our heads dinged as the streetlight turned red and the bridge gates lowered. The boat's passengers stopped talking and turned toward the bridge. I followed their gazes, the sun at our backs, the freeway traffic above our heads sounding like waves crashing against a rocky shore. In the stroller, Helen sighed and slept and grew older while I stood by the water's edge near a group of strangers, suspended in time and space, our heads tilted upward as we waited for the two halves of the bridge to part from one another and make their slow ascent.

# 27. Pre-Race

Seventy-nine days after Beth died, I sat on the floor of the Marriott in Monterey, California, laying out my clothes for the Pacific Grove Triathlon the next morning. I placed the body-less version of myself on the floor, shorts atop shoes, singlet race jersey above shorts. At the foot of the bed I made three piles: swim, bike, run. I checked items off the Team in Training-issued packing list as I moved them from the pile to my backpack: goggles, wetsuit, running hat. I slid four energy bars into the pack's front pocket and carried my Camelback water pack, full and dripping, from the bathroom to my spot on the floor. An anthill-sized pile of safety pins sat on the bed, and I picked them up one by one as I pinned a photograph of Beth in her kayak onto my Camelback.

The fourteen other members of my Team in Training group were performing the same packing rituals in their own hotel rooms. Ande, the captain of the Lavaman Team, had moved up to the role of coach for Pacific Grove. I was the third oldest member of the team and I felt out of place in the group, spit-up on my workout clothes and eyes rimmed red from sleep deprivation. My slowness stuck out more there than it had in the Lavaman group, and I was always dead last on our bikes and runs. Our family schedule meant that I had to skip practice a lot, but I preferred to train on my own anyway. I often retreated to the gym, which had the dual luxuries of air conditioning and a child care room.

As I pinned my race number to my singlet, a sinking feeling overcame me. In Seattle I'd failed to purchase a race belt, in the "optional" column on the packing list, but recommended. In a triathlon, racers have their numbers displayed three different ways. For the swim, volunteer "body markers" write the number on racers' limbs with a grease pen or ink stamp. Your bike's top tube gets a stickered number, and you receive a paper version for the run. This paper number gets attached to the race belt. After the bike, wet-shirted and in a hurry, you simply clip the belt around your waist and go.

I'd never used a race belt. It seemed unnecessary, an item for hard-core racers only. In my previous races, I'd worn a loose t-shirt that slid easily over my wet body post-swim, my run number pinned to the front. Team in Training wanted us to wear the snug-fitting singlet, though, special ordered and stamped with their logo and sponsors. In the hotel room I practiced putting it on. Even with a dry body, I struggled to get it on, the paper race number buckling and threatening to tear. If Matt had been there, he would have come up with a solution to my problem, MacGyvered something into place. I missed him. I missed the kids. I missed Beth.

In the time since Beth had died, Helen had learnt to roll over and sit up. At six months her reflux had vanished and she smiled constantly. She still hadn't grown hair or teeth, and her cheeks were disproportionately large. She looked like the baby on the front of the food jars we'd soon be feeding her from.

Caleb, not yet two-and-a-half, ran faster than he talked. He smiled a lot too, but he'd been in a tantrum-y phase the past few months, the kicking and screaming kind that, when done in public, caused people to shoot angry or sympathetic looks at Matt and me. He'd started preschool the week before the race, and I worried that my absence, though only three days long, would accentuate any anxieties he may have had about spending his days in an unfamiliar child care setting. He'd been fine, though, when I'd left for the airport.

Alone in the hotel, I allowed my grief about Beth to release from it's normally tamped-down state. My skin felt as though it had been painted with pottery glaze and my senses vacillated like a fever spiking then subsiding. One minute I'd feel numb, the next the edges of everything felt too sharp. No one could see the bowling ball on my chest, but I sensed it shallowing my breaths.

In truth, I did not know how to do the race in Beth's memory. Should I hold her in my mind's eye and talk to her? I did that anyway, every time I went for a run or a bike ride. Midnights, rocking Helen back to sleep after a feeding, I'd look out the window at the inky sky, the night-lighted city, and carry on a one-way conversation with Beth. How do we do this, any of it, without you?

\*\*\*

At the registration table earlier that day, I'd learnt the atypical way Pacific Grove would be organized. The race consisted of wave starts according to reverse age, as usual, but the elites would go last instead of first. Sandwiched between the age groupers and the pros would be special Team in Training waves. As an over-thirty-five-year-old woman, I'd be in the last start wave. There would be a time-gap before the elites started their race. Not long enough, I thought, for me to be finished cycling before the course closed.

"I won't be finished biking by noon," I told the registration volunteer, a short, stocky woman in her mid-sixties. She smiled reassuringly.

"You just have to be on the bike course by then," she said. "You'd have to be really slow to still be in the water at noon."

If I'd been in the regular age group wave instead of the Team in Training one, I'd have more time before the cut-off. I should have asked the volunteer to move me, an adjustment that would have only required a switch to a different coloured swim cap. But I was ignorant about race logistics. Or maybe I simply lacked assertiveness. Still, after all I'd been through.

"Don't worry about it," Ande said when I told him about my start time. "You'll be faster than you think. And if you aren't, your team will have your back."

But I wouldn't be with the team. I'd be racing against the clock. Precise, perfect time. Neither punishing nor forgiving. Time would not slow down or stop the way it often seemed to do. It would simply keep going, seconds, minutes, hours, one after the other. My only choice then, the only choice I'd ever had, was to move forward along with it, no matter what happened.

# 28. Personal Record

A triathlon starts with a swim, they say, to lessen the likelihood of fatigue-induced drowning. Photographs of the Northern California race location did not imply risk: tropical fish gliding through clear, serene waters under a cloudless sky. But race day dawned in a chilly mist. Kayakers bobbed on four-foot swells around the course perimeter, and the rescue boat hunched in the middle of the course plucked two seasick swimmers out of the gunmetal sea.

Clad in a lilac cap and a taut wetsuit, my goggles already fogging, I approached the first buoy. One hundred of us swam in each group, clustered by age and gender, identically costumed. From above we might've looked like a dragon from a Chinese New Year parade, the long, sprawling tail decorated with purple rubber balls. As we worked our way around the triangular course, we choked on fifty-eight degree seawater, arms tangled in noodles of brown kelp, turning our heads for breath after breath. We kicked each other with numbed feet, knocking bodies as we scrabbled for a good position.

I rounded the second race buoy and my shoulders relaxed. Every third or fourth stroke I hit a patch of kelp; I yanked on its rubbery edges and swam through it. A quarter-mile from the beach, I accelerated and began passing other racers. I'd never passed anyone swimming, in a race or otherwise. I'm racing, I thought. I'm fast.

When my hands hit the sand I stood and jogged toward

the beach, barely outrunning an oncoming wave. I felt lightheaded and disoriented by the cheering crowd and the music blaring through the loudspeaker. I climbed the hill to the transition area, my legs wobbling. Sea legs. But I was on dry land. My strongest of the three sports, finished. At the finish line behind me, a digital clock ticked away the hours, minutes, seconds in giant lime-green numerals. Hurry up, it seemed to be saying. You're running out of time.

My watch read 10:17 as I arrived, dizzy and panting, at my designated spot in the transition area. Ande stood to the side of the bike rack, and grinned when he saw me.

"How was the swim?" he said.

"Good," I said. "I made it through the kelp." I reached behind my head and found the zipper pull with my hands, still velcroed to my wetsuit near the nape of my neck. I unzipped the back and peeled it partway off, stopping below my sports bra. I looked down to make sure my shorts still covered my colostomy pouch. I picked up the hand towel from beside my shoes and wiped my face and torso. Between the sea water and the spitting rain, I would never be able to get dry as long as I remained outside.

I dropped my towel, picked up my singlet, and pulled it over my head. I put my arms in the arm holes and tugged. I got past my bra, and then the shirt stuck. I twisted my body circus contortionist-style, I rolled the fabric at the bottom of my shirt. I tugged. I heard the sound of fabric ripping.

"You lost a safety pin," Ande said, coming around from the other side of the bike rack to help me locate it in the grass. Coaches were allowed to help racers in the transition area for a maximum of thirty seconds, an official race rule. He handed me the pin and walked back to his spot on the other side of the rack. I re-pinned the corner of my number. The whole process must have taken five minutes. I still had to put on my socks, my lace-up shoes, my bike helmet.

"Guess I should buy a race belt," I said.

"It's worth the eight bucks," Ande said.

Two teammates from my start wave ran up to their spots beside me at the rack and I greeted them as I walked over to the Porta Potty. When I emerged one of them was already gone, the other clipping her bike helmet under her chin as I ran to the gate, pushing my bike alongside me like a horse I was coaxing out of its stable.

*** 

Despite the fact that I am afraid of bicycles, that I'm slow, that my technique lacks finesse, I never panic during the bike portion of a race. Often, in fact, it's the highpoint of the day, the moment where I say: How about that? Not so long ago, I was so sick and weak from surgery I could barely walk. Now I'm in a triathlon. I'm a racer. I'm an athlete.

At Pacific Grove, riders passed me frequently: ascending, descending, on the flat stretches. The narrow two-lane was full of riders calling out to one another, others with their heads down in perfect aerodynamic position. Many of the riders wore Team in Training gear, a sea of purple among the fluorescent jerseys. I rode my hybrid, its upright handlebars putting me in a good viewing position.

"It's the bike's fault," my Lavaman teammate had said during my first running practice when I told him I was a slow rider. I'd passed up the bike prize from my top fundraiser status at Lavaman, a triathlon bike that was light and built for racing. Would I be riding faster if I were on that bike?

I checked my watch. 11:50. Two minutes later I approached the turnaround for my last lap, past a throng of people yelling loudly at their family members and friends. I looked for Ande, who'd been standing at this corner the entire time, calling my name and whistling each time I passed. I didn't see him. He'd probably gone to the run course to cheer on my teammates. I steered toward the turn.

And that's when it happened.

I saw the black mesh barricade in front of me; on the other side, the mat I needed to tag, the stretch of road ahead. I thought of the craggy rocks, more visible with each lap as the fog retreated, the Beachcomber Inn with its Best Summer Rates sign at the top of the final hill, far in the distance. I was supposed to pass those landmarks one more time, finish my protein bar, drain my water pack.

***

"I have one more lap to do," I yelled to one of the arm-wavers.

"You won't have time," she called back, pointing toward the course exit. The first elite athlete emerged from the transition area and climbed onto his bike. He wouldn't be on an empty course at all. Hundreds of non-professionals remained on the road, including my teammate who'd passed me five minutes before. Five minutes. If only I'd swum a little faster, pedalled a little harder. If only I'd bought a race belt, I'd have made the turn before they closed the course.

Instead, my forward progress was grinding to a halt. Another interruption, just like my stitches tearing open, my failed pregnancy attempts, Beth's death. Everything, it seemed, happened to me out of order, and not at all how I'd planned it. The barricade stretched across the road like a boulder plunked in the middle of the river I'd been paddling down. Unlike the other road blocks I'd faced, there was no going around this one.

I dismounted onto rubbery legs and began jogging, slowing to a walk as I entered the transition area. My bike tires bumped over the lawn until I reached the rack. Don't cry, I told myself. The act of holding back tears made my movements abrupt and jerky, the manoeuvres of a young child who has lost the last game of the season. I hoisted my front wheel over the rack, removed my helmet and let the nylon strap slide out of my hand. It hit the rack once with a *thwap* before landing on the grass.

I took a breath and slid my Camelback off my shoulders, taking time to face Beth's photo upwards. I picked up my running hat and waist pack. The pack held a spare colostomy pouch, a sleeve of energy chews, and a water bottle, none of which I would need, all of which felt necessary to take along as planned. I used the Porta Potty, stepping over the discarded toilet paper roll cores to hover above the urine-spattered toilet seat.

I wove my way across the transition area toward the sign marked Run Start. The lawn was crowded with racers, younger, faster people who started before me and were already done. They laughed, snapped photos, ate the race-provided lunch from paper plates. They'd zipped jackets over their chiselled torsos to get warm, careful to display their finishers medals on the outside of their coats. I reached the opening in the fence, the thought bubble above my head crammed with curse words. Time to start running.

\*\*\*

"Are you on your second lap or your third?" A woman asked as she ran past me, her blonde hair tucked in a still-tidy ponytail.

"My first," I said through gritted teeth. I added her to my list of People I Hate Right Now, immediately below the race director, the elite athletes, and all of the people I asked about the course closure who told me not to worry. I thought of the time I'd spent—a year—preparing for that day. All for nothing.

Race volunteers stood every half mile with Dixie cups of water and Powerade. I'd just passed the fourth water stop when I felt someone's hand clamp down on my shoulder, pushing me forward. I turned and saw a man who, his attention on his own water-grab, did not see me.

"Sorry," he called behind him, already past me. He wore a pro-athlete unitard. It was one of the elite competitors, the one who would go on to win the entire race. I got off the bike course for him, and then he tried to run me over.

Surrounded by thousands of people in the triathlon, I felt a surge of loneliness. My only companionship since my feet hit the water hours before had been the imaginary conversation I'd carried on with Beth.

I gave myself a pep talk. Remember goal number three, Enjoy Yourself? You're failing. I tried looking on the bright side. My legs didn't ache as much after nineteen miles of riding as they would if I'd done the full twenty-five. I wouldn't be the last person to cross the finish line. I thought of all I'd done, and tried to be proud of my accomplishments. But the pride felt forced, the victory hollow. I came to do the whole distance, just like everyone else. And now I wouldn't get to. I hadn't stood up for myself back on the bike course. I could have talked to a race official then, showed her the time on my watch, the premature placement of the barricade. It's what Beth would have done. Hadn't I learnt anything from her?

We ran on a concrete boardwalk lined with tourist shops

and restaurants. On the road above people ambled by, as though no race was taking place. I had that feeling I'd had during my first running practice nearly a year before, where I considered going home. Then, among the sea of unrecognizable spectators, I saw a teammate. He was tall and pointy-nosed with black hair cut in a square-ish style. He'd been a barefoot runner before it was trendy, racing in the kind of flimsy shoes people use to wade in rock-bottomed shallows. He stood with his wife, his backpack slung over his hunched shoulder. He didn't look elated, as I thought he should. His smile seemed strained. He'd had his own bike course mishap, I'd find out later. He misunderstood the route, and stopped after two laps instead of completing all four. His expression brightened when he saw me.

"Go Janet! Goooo!" he yelled, like we were old friends. It was the most animated I'd ever seen him. I assumed he would have left for the hotel by the time I came back around, but he was there for my second lap, and my third.

As I passed him a final time, I made a decision, and my mind settled for the first time that day. I accelerated, and thought of Ande's running advice from our track practices. For those last yards, my feet struck the pavement mid-arch, my stride quick as though I ran on hot lava. I crossed the finish line. No alarm went off. The volunteer on my left removed my timing chip and handed me a bottle of water. The one on my right beamed at me.

"Congratulations," she said. I bent my head forward and she placed the finisher's medal around my neck.

\*\*\*

I walked past the still-celebrating crowd to my bike. I fished my jacket out of my pack and zipped it over my race jersey, tucking my finisher's medal in my pocket. I clipped my helmet strap around my chin and walked my bike to the edge of the road. I found a volunteer and explained what had happened on the bike course. Sometimes standing up for yourself means waiting for the right moment to make your voice heard.

"I have six more miles to ride," I said. "Can I do them now?" She told me to wait until the road cleared of everyone else: racers, officials, the teenagers with their cowbells and party horns.

"Remove your race number from your bike and helmet," she said. "Cover up the Team in Training logo on your shirt." I couldn't be mistaken for a racer, and risk causing alarm. I needed to look like someone out for a leisurely afternoon ride.

I left my water pack with Beth's picture in the transition area, next to my wetsuit and running hat. The grass was littered with disposable water bottles and half-empty energy gel packs. Ande looked over from across the lawn where he was posing for a photo with my teammates. I'd seen him at the finish line and told him my plan. Though I didn't ask him to, at the end of my ride I'd find him standing in the transition area, waiting for me to return.

\*\*\*

The final lap turned out to be my favourite. I thought it would feel like a consolation prize, the post-race ride. Instead, it felt like a victory lap. It was my own private triathlon; for the first time that day I enjoyed the feeling of solitude. The lump in my throat dissolved. The rain had stopped, and through the retreating mist I saw cormorants and gulls bobbing on the water. Underneath them I could picture seals swimming, their sleek bodies following a northward path parallel to my own on the other side of the outcropping of rocks.

The miles passed as my focus shifted from the race to what I would order from room service when I got back to the hotel to imagining Caleb's and Helen's faces when they greeted me at the airport the next afternoon. I thought about Beth. For the first time since her death, the image that came to my mind was not her unconscious body in bed the day before she died. It was of her laughing, something she'd done in nearly every interaction I'd had with her. I loved her laugh, a three-noted sound that ascended in octaves as it progressed.

A year before, when she'd called after my triathlon to tell me the cancer had come back, she'd laughed on the phone as I told her about the teenage girl I'd met early on the run course, the one who'd lost thirty pounds over the summer. After a few minutes of running together, I told Beth, the girl slowed down, telling me to go ahead. When I saw her again at the final water stop, she was limping, barely running. She told me her ankle hurt.

"Maybe you should walk," I said.

"No," she said, picking up her pace. "I trained all summer. I am running this whole fucking race."

And she did. She matched my strides for the last mile, pulling ahead of me when the cheering crowd came in sight. Confused by the course, she veered right, away from the finish line. I yelled to her and she looped back, running past the finish line, past the race volunteers collecting timing chips, stopping only when she reached her family at the end of the barricade.

Beth's death from cancer had been sudden, a fact that still shocked me months later. She'd gone from the Swiss Alps to hospice care in the space of a week. The end came too quickly for all of us. Except Beth, of course. Surely she wanted that last stretch to be as short as possible: the pain, the struggle to speak, to move her limbs, to breathe. Maybe she even brought on her own swift ending by force of will. I can imagine her internal conversation, punctuated with a final, triumphant line. *I am running this whole fucking race.*

# 29. Sitka

We moved the box containing Beth's ashes around her house like it was a boa constrictor in a glass tank. Don't let it out of sight, make sure it stays in a warm room, and never, ever put it on the floor.

I'd come to help pack. Kevin was moving back to his hometown, Sitka, Alaska, population 9,000. Sixteen miles from one end of town to the other, a narrow strip of streets sandwiched between the Gulf of Alaska and the Tongass National Forest. Ravens and eagles competed for air space above the town's two stoplights, the shell-littered beaches, the fishery, the brewery, the park where Beth and Kevin got married, and the library with a commanding view of the marina.

Kevin bought a piece of land and planned to build himself a house amid the stand of yellow cedars. On winter evenings, he'd skate on the lake near the high school with his nephews, their blades bumping over the ice, their breath dragoning out of their mouths in tiny clouds. In summertime he'd take the boys down to the docks to buy crabs from the boats that pulled in every afternoon, the sun still sitting in the centre of the sky, waiting until midnight to set.

Matt and I were fixing up our house too; rather, we'd hired builders to renovate it for us. The three-bedroom rental we lived in during construction had a larger footprint than our house would have, post-renovation. Still, it felt crowded and disorganized, our clothes stuffed in closets, unpaid bills and house schematics stacked in haphazard piles on shelves. Evenings, I tried to find our missing belongings: my cycling gloves and Matt's ski goggles. Our favourite bedtime story, *Owl Moon*, inscribed by a childhood friend of Caleb's birthmom Bree. Helen was ready to use the bouncer that hung in the doorway, the one that entertained Caleb for hours as a baby, but I couldn't locate it. I went down to the basement with a flashlight, searching through the same boxes over and over, lifting our camping tent, our life jackets, as though something might appear that was not there before.

\*\*\*

My first packing assignment: Beth's books. Hundreds filled their house, an Augusten Burroughs memoir, a Federico Garcia Lorca poetry collection, several titles from the women's studies classes Beth took in college. Not a trashy novel in sight. I arranged stacks in three boxes, labelled Giveaway, Storage, and Going North. This was how Kevin referred to Sitka, as though he was an explorer moving to a distant, unmapped land. In fact, Sitka is only 850 miles from Seattle. One can get there in an hour and a half by aeroplane, or, according to a boat rental shop in Seattle, six to eight weeks by kayak. Kevin reserved a spot for himself on the ferry from Bellingham. It would be a three-day boat trip.

"I want to be near the front of the line," Kevin told me, "so I can get a foldout chair on the sun deck."

We talked about Sitka over lunch. Every time I went to pack, we walked to the Husky Deli around the corner to get our shared favourite cuisine: sandwiches. Southwest chicken for me, grilled veggie for Kevin. Kevin varied his order, perhaps wanting to sample his favourites before heading to Sitka. I always ordered the same sandwich. I waited in line, wedged between an overweight man on his cell phone and a candy display. The mint chocolate cookies beckoned me from the silver-lidded glass jar at the register. Beth loved chocolate. I was trying to cut back.

I could've stopped with the books, the files. I was busy with parenting, with the remodel, with running our household. The kids took 100 percent of my time, and then some, their needs simultaneously basic and bottomless: play dates, potty training, solid food introduction, train-track construction. But I kept returning. Not because Kevin asked me to; I volunteered for the job. I went half a dozen times. I put in six-hour shifts while the kids were with the babysitter. I was obsessed. I told myself it gave me space to grieve, to say goodbye. But I wasn't saying goodbye. I was clinging.

I packed Beth's baby teeth, her jewellery, her half-used deodorant stick. I didn't know we used the same brand. In the bedroom, I found a box containing Catholic figurines Beth must've received as a child, a tiny Virgin Mary and one labelled Saint Elizabeth in pale blue lettering. I lifted them out of the box to encase them in bubble wrap. Underneath the figurines lay a plaster moulding of a hand, 1974 etched on the backside. Beth's three-year-old hand, its size somewhere between Helen's and Caleb's. I sat still for a minute or an hour, cradling the moulding in my palm, before putting it back in the box. The falsetto squeak of Kevin's tape gun echoed through the house, the throb of rap music downstairs vibrated the floorboards underneath my knees.

One day I pulled a grocery bag off the closet shelf, its

plastic stretched and lumpy from the contents. Dozens of prescription bottles filled the bag. I found Kevin in the kitchen, packing spices.

"Want me to get rid of these for you?" I said. He reached into the bag and began pulling out bottles. Anti-seizure drugs. Prednisone. Morphine. Kevin said we couldn't flush them down the toilet. I suggested getting a hammer and pulverizing each individual Prednisone pill.

"Or we could go out onto the street corner," he said. "Make ourselves some money." He pawed through the bag, pulling out bottles to read labels and speculate which ones would fetch the best price. We laughed, and then fell quiet. I could hear cars pulling into the hardware store parking lot across the street, the beep of a contractor's van backing up. Kevin opened the refrigerator and pulled out a packet of pills.

"Oral chemo," he said, tossing it into the bag. "Worthless."

"I'll take care of it," I said, pulling the bag away from him. I felt strong at that moment, like I would have no problem carrying a huge bag full of my dead friend's drugs up to the pharmacy window and dropping it on the counter. But I couldn't. Instead, I enlisted our houseguest. He returned from the pharmacy that evening with the liquid morphine, the only item the drug store employees would not dispense of themselves.

"They said to mix it with cat litter and throw it in the trash," our friend told Matt and me as we cleaned up after dinner. I looked at Matt across the kitchen island.

"I'll do it," Matt said, drying his hands on a dishtowel and descending the stairs to the basement where we kept our Mingus' supplies. I continued washing Helen's baby bottles, my back to the rest of the house, the rinse water too hot.

\*\*\*

I went over to the house a final time, a few days before Kevin moved to Sitka. He'd be spending most of the day getting his new truck rigged with ladder racks and a top for the bed, to fit his new house-builder persona. The iPod was on when I arrived, and I was grateful for the noise. This would be my first time in the house alone, ever.

I walked down the hallway, and peeked my head into the place I'd been avoiding, the room where Beth died. A broom was propped against the wall in one corner, a roll of packing tape beside it on the floor. Underneath one window, the white pine box containing Beth's ashes sat on a small table. At her service I'd watched her brother rest his open palm on the lid of the box. I walked over to the table and did the same, taking shallow gulps of breath while my hand touched the wood.

If Matt died, what would my Sitka be? Would I move back to the East Coast, a place I found socially oppressive, to be near my family? Would I take the kids somewhere new for a fresh start, someplace not littered with memories of Matt? Somewhere that sounded as cool as Sitka: Missoula, Montana. Pocatello, Idaho. Burnt Creek, Georgia. Matt and I had dreams for the house renovation, a roof-deck covered in native plants, a steam shower, and bookcases built into every available wall. Maybe the new house, its reinforced walls painted in soothing yellows and greens, would be strong enough to hold me through a loss I couldn't fathom.

I walked to the deli. I considered a different sandwich, but then "southwest chicken" came out of my mouth as the cashier stood, waiting. Giving in at last, I picked up the plastic tongs and retrieved a mint chocolate cookie from the glass jar by the register. As I waited for my order, I wondered if Sitka had a good enough deli to meet Kevin's needs. Did he have someone there to share his love of sandwiches? Maybe this was something we would lament, the lack of a local sandwich companion, when we sat in our respective houses in different states and talked on the phone.

After Beth died, I called Kevin more than I ever had when she was alive, to extend a dinner invitation or just to check in. One evening while out of town, my grief poking especially sharply at the borders of my heart, I phoned.

"Hello," he said, his voice full of recognition and cheer. He giggled. Was he drunk?

"What are you doing?" I said.

"Watching *Bill and Ted's Excellent Adventure*." This would have been a forbidden act if Beth was alive and at home, as would the giant flat-screen television he bought a week after she died. I laughed back.

\*\*\*

"It feels like losing Beth all over again," I said to Matt when I returned from packing one day.

"But Kevin isn't dying," Matt said. "He's just moving. We could visit him in Sitka," Matt said. Kevin would make trips to Seattle. Matt was right. Time to say goodbye.

\*\*\*

Back at the house on the final packing day, Kevin had moved the dining room table into the storage room. I ate at the kitchen counter, looking out onto the garden. I'd stood in the dirt with Beth one afternoon as she described their vision of plants of different heights and colours.

"It will look cool when it's all established," she said.

"Lush, but not overgrown." She'd given the perfect description.

I washed my dish with a frayed sponge that smelt of expired food. I dried the plate with a towel before folding it in bubble wrap, and placing it in the Rubbermaid container on the floor. I ingested the cookie, spreading crumbs on the floor that I later swept up. I did not savour every bite.

# 30. The Mountain

In a private summertime ceremony, Beth's family scattered her ashes under a cedar in Mount Rainier National Park. On a weekday in December two years after her death, while Caleb was at preschool and Helen was with a babysitter, I drove south to the Paradise Visitor's centre parking lot.

I didn't have to live in Seattle long to understand the role that Rainier plays in its residents' lives. The backdrop to our city, it dangles from an invisible chain, a locket containing shards of memories, hopes, failures. Native Americans first knew Rainier as Tahoma, meaning "mother of waters." Local waterways are fed by snowmelt from twenty-six glaciers. These days, we refer to it simply as "The Mountain." Often, clouds obscure our view of it as it rises over 14,000 feet from the ground. During its visible moments, we Seattleites slow our cars on the freeway to take a long look. I like to watch the setting sun pinken the glaciers, the summit's tip transforming into a watercolour, fading until it's indistinguishable from the night sky.

\*\*\*

Dozens of families clustered a few hundred feet above Paradise Lodge, taking turns skidding downhill on sleds as I strapped on my snowshoes. Once I reached trees, I had the trail to myself, the crunch of my snowshoes and my exhales of breath the only sounds in the world. I stopped to gaze at the mountain's snow-covered face and the steel-blue underside of its glaciers.

That day marked my first solo snowshoe and my first time visiting Rainier by myself. In my lifetime, I'd rarely been alone. I'd never lived without housemates or gone on a solo trip. I could count on one hand the number of hikes I'd done without someone else. Part of it was the fear of getting lost or hurt with no one around to help me. Part of it was discomfort at the idea of my own thoughts jangling around in my head. I needed a constant companion, I believed, to test out my ideas, to reassure myself that I was on the right track.

By the time of my snowshoe trip, though, I'd walked several solo paths: illness, infertility, miscarriage. It felt as though Beth's death, premature and sudden as it was, had knocked loose any last threads of dependence. Now I longed to be alone, because it meant no one needed anything from me: their sippy cup filled, their diaper changed. Being by myself meant I could let my thoughts spool out uninterrupted. I could talk to Beth in my head.

I crested a rise and there it was, the size of a helicopter pad, the section of trail known as the "dance floor." I made my way to Beth's cedar, which stood at the edge of the flat portion of the trail. Wind had carved the snow into a perfectly circular bowl around the tree, deep enough to expose its roots.

I'd visited Rainier with Beth once. A year after I moved to Seattle, we'd gone on a day hike with two other work friends.

"If there's a trail between earth and heaven," Beth read from the guide book while we drove to the park, "this is it." I remember the four of us laughing inside the car. Heaven did not interest us. We just wanted to spend the day outside. That had been in late summer, the lower slopes of the mountain still blanketed in green and marmots popping up from behind rocks.

My snowshoe trip took place a week before the winter solstice, Beth's birthday. The word solstice comes from the Latin *sol* (sun) and *sistere* (to stand still), because on those days the seasonal movement of the sun stops briefly before reversing direction. Forty years earlier, Beth's parents had driven through a Chicago snowstorm to the hospital. Early in the morning on the winter solstice, their first child and only daughter was born. They named her Elizabeth Clare, a good Catholic name. Elizabeth, meaning "worshiper of God." Clare after her father's sister who would become a favourite aunt. Beth's wintry beginnings formed an early love of snow. She was always the last to come inside from an afternoon of sledding, a habit that earned her the nickname "Bear."

At the cedar I'd envisioned sharing anecdotes in a loud voice punctuated with laughter. But that was Beth's voice, not mine. I inhaled deeply, blowing all my breath out at once.

"Happy Birthday," I said.

\*\*\*

When Beth was sick, I tried sometimes to imagine how it would be after she died, what it would feel like to miss her. Then, I thought I knew what it felt like to have her removed from my life. It would be like the eight months we did not speak. I missed her then. So many times I wanted to talk to her. But I thought she'd left me, moved onto other friends. I did not know that my absence created a hole for Beth, too. I was unaware until Kevin told me, after she died.

"Do you notice something missing from our lives?" Beth

had said to him one day during those eight months.

"What do you mean?" Kevin asked.

"Janet and Matt," she said. "I don't know what happened there."

I know what happened. We thought we had time to grow apart, to come back together. I thought, then, that I knew what it was like to lose a friend.

But it wasn't like that at all, with her across town, my phone quiet on the hall table. It was—it still is—a different kind of silence: our living room absent of Beth's voice, Caleb and Helen unfamiliar with the sound of her laugh or the size of her hands as she flew them, aeroplane-style, around our back yard. She would have attended their soccer games and choir concerts. She would have joined the circle of stuffed animals assembled for the tea party on the playroom floor.

Where was Beth at that moment, two years after the scattering? If we continue on in some form after we die, maybe she was still by her cedar, or maybe she'd flown south for the winter. Maybe she visited more than one place at once, soaring with the eagles and ravens above the Sitka beach, sunbathing at the park while her nieces played softball, dangling inside the water drops that cling to a grizzly's fur when she wades into the river to take a drink.

\*\*\*

Grief is not a temporary state nor a demon we can exorcize. It's more like a skin we wear inside our own. Eventually it blends into our body, becoming a part of our being that we carry with us always. We learn to live with it, to bear it. Beth became a piece of this new skin, her essence helping hold our broken parts together. I'd lost so much—babies and body parts and a dear friend. These events had flattened me in every sense, requiring me to remain horizontal, or making it hard to get out of bed. But I did, every morning, from the first day after the first surgery onward. I stood up for myself. I stood up. I stood.

I stood by Beth's tree in silence while time passed without me noticing it. The sun made the snow look like an ice rink. The sky appeared as a painter's tint sample, blue-black at the top of the horizon, cobalt in the middle, pale blue where it grazed the tops of distant peaks, flat-topped Mt. St. Helen's and its pointy-hatted neighbours.

The hike with Beth all those years ago had been the same cloudless weather. Despite our desire to avoid thoughts of the afterlife, during our lunch stop we agreed that the guidebook was right. We'd left the earth for someplace celestial. It was otherworldly, this brown swath of trail forming a ladder to the shiny, ice-encrusted mountaintop.

And it was heavenly again as I stood in my snowshoes, wanting to stay, ready to go. I lingered there, the mountain a giant beacon, beckoning. I shouldered my pack. I turned toward the cedar, nodding my head in a silent goodbye. I began my descent.

Not wanting to disturb the settled feelings within me, I left the stereo off as I exited the parking lot and descended the windy road. A fox ran across the pavement a few hundred feet in front of my car and I pressed my foot onto the brake longer than necessary, watching the fox's scrub-brush tail disappear behind a snow bank. As I left the park and drove through gradually larger towns, the terrain changed from evergreen-dotted snow to bare trees and fallow fields. I passed a casino and an outdoor concert venue. I pulled over and turned to gaze at The Mountain once more.

If the death of a loved one leaves an immeasurable hole,

the rawness of loss creating a scooped-out place inside of us, then Rainier is grief's opposite, rising out of planed farmland, its summit so high it often disappears into the clouds.

***

Two hours after I left the park, I arrived home. We'd lived in our renovated house a year by then, but I still marvelled at its improvements—our eat-in kitchen, the upstairs deck that overlooked a flat roof covered in lavender, salal, and native grasses. The builders used sustainable materials throughout the house. Items diverted from the waste pile became countertops, built-in dressers. Diseased walnut trees, their tumours removed, stood proudly in their new role as kitchen cabinets.

With most of its parts replaced, is it the same house we lived in before? I still grieve in our house. The dead remain dead. But the sadness feels sanded down. Beth returned to the house with us. I picture her standing in our L-shaped kitchen, chopping vegetables on the built-in cutting board. The house re-orients me. It captures new memories.

As I walk inside, four-year-old Caleb and two-year-old Helen run to the door to greet me like puppies. Matt stands in the kitchen, calling a soft hello as he fixes dinner. Time has warped since my early morning departure. The kids seem older than when I left and it feels like I've been gone much longer than half a day. Long enough, perhaps, to appreciate our time together anew. We have the remainder of this evening and the thousands that will follow. We'll measure their progress through marks on the growth chart in the hallway, and the displaying of artwork and sports trophies and photographs from the dance recital. Time will continue to unfold this way, slowing and accelerating of its own accord.

Caleb shows me the tiger cave he created from couch cushions in our hallway. Helen pulls me towards the stereo. I know what she wants, so I put in the CD and forward to the right song. "Yellow Submarine." All four of us sing and Helen chimes in with the words she knows: *we all live*. I turn the music up loud, and in the living room, we dance.

# Acknowledgements

I could not have written one word of this without all of the gutsy people in my life, who support me and provide wonderful examples of how to be brave on and off the page. Enormous gratitude to:

Ana Maria Spagna, my advisor, teacher, mentor, and friend, who coached me through every twist and turn and showed me how to write with courage. The entire rest of the crew at the Northwest Institute of Literary Arts, including faculty members Larry Cheek, Bruce Holland Rogers, and Melissa Hart for their wisdom and generosity. Fellow students formed my original writing tribe, and offered friendship, feedback, and support: Erika Brumett, Jeremiah O'Hagan, Iris Graville, Claire Gebben, Sandy Sarr, Jackie Haskins, Stephanie Barbe Hammer, (honorary member) Larry Behrendt, Christine Myers, Stefon Mears, Andy Sieple, YiShun Lai, Chels Knorr, Francis Wood, Stefanie Freele, Tanya Chernov, Kelly Davio, Kim Lundstrom, and Deborah Nedelman.

Those who read the manuscript – in part and in whole, often multiple times - and offered essential feedback: Chad Marsh, Amanda Skelton, Theo Nestor, Jane Friedman, Marin Younker, the Flick Creek crew, Tracy Strauss, Judith Sara Gelt, Ryan Lurie, Georgia Hunter, Jon Lasser, Alicia Craven, Kristina Keogh.

Jessica Bell, Peter Snell, Lindsay Adkins, and the entire team at Vine Leaves Press for their belief in the manuscript and for their championing of first-time authors.

Brian Doyle, for his enthusiasm for everything, including

GUTS, and for filling the world with his words before his too-soon departure from it. I'm honoured to have had his quote of support while I was finding a home for my manuscript, and grateful to have known him.

Leigh Stein, Sonya Huber, and Nicole Hardy for the honour of including their quotes on my book jacket.

Jennie Shortridge and the staff and members of Seattle-7Writers for awarding me the 2017 Sorting Room Residency and providing the perfect space to finish the manuscript.

Thanks also to the Brumett family, Chris Steck, Venue, for additional writing spaces.

Brian McGuigan and the staff at Richard Hugo House in Seattle, for providing me with my first teaching home. The faculty and staff of the Tin House Summer Writers' Workshop for multiple summers spent working on GUTS, with special thanks to Team Jess Walter for the best entrée into fiction writing a memoirist could hope for.

The medical professionals who took care of me, with special thanks to the world's greatest ostomy nurse, Laura Vadman.

The people who take care of my children with love, patience, and care while I write: Chloe Shaw, Emily Delahunty, Nick Terrones, Kristin Meyer, the teaching staff at Hilltop Children's Center, and the wonderful staff and teachers at Hamlin Robinson School. Special thanks to my mother-in-law, Sylvia Watkins-Castillo, for coming to Seattle while I retreated to Whidbey Island for my writing residencies.

The Petermans and the Knoxes, for sharing their hearts and their Beautiful Beth.

To my family, for everything: my parents Katie & Paul Buttenwieser, my siblings Susan & Stephen Buttenwieser, their partners Andy Blackman & Rachel Harrington-Levey.

My other families, original and adopted: The Wileys,

The Watkins-Castillos, The Tesfus, for your support of all of my endeavors, writing and otherwise. The CC Crowd, with special thanks to Amy Edwards for co-organization, feeding, listening, advising, and other marks of enduring friendship.

I began writing this book in 2009 at age 38, the year that Beth died. Then that seemed an impossibly young age for life to end. Now I'm 46, a time we define as middle-aged. I wish the fact of its middle-ness could somehow be warranteed for everyone. But Beth was only the first friend gone too young. In fond remembrance of the others who died during the course of writing this book, co-workers and friends, biological and honorary family members: David Johnson, Roberto Enriquez, Toni Botello, Mark Lane, Sam Shepard, Jill Buttenwieser, Marsh McCall. To my friends who've lost someone close to them: *I'm sorry for your loss* doesn't begin to express it. Thank you for opening your hearts to me and making my grieving process a less lonely one.

Kevin Knox, for showing us how to follow Beth's directive to live life out loud. Thank you for sharing memories and giving me the space and support to tell the story my own way. Here's to many, many more sandwiches.

Caleb & Helen Wiley, you are my sunshine.

And finally, enormous love and gratitude to Matt Wiley for combining your change with mine for the best-ever 7-11 run. This is only the latest of my complicated endeavors, none of which I could have done without you by my side. Thank you for being an unflappable, gentle, humour-filled companion.

# Publication
# Acknowledgements

Some chapters in GUTS were originally published as essays, often in a different form. Thank you to the editors of the following journals for giving these words their first homes: *The Rumpus* ("Out of Order," June 2016); *Under the Sun* ("Laws of Motion," 2015); *The Pinch* ("Pins and Needles," October 2014); *Stymie* ("Personal Record," October 2014); *Potomac Review* ("Chief Complaint," Winter 2013); *Mason's Road* ("Running Out the Clock," Winter 2013); *Shark Reef* ("Approved for Occupancy," Summer 2012); *Bellevue Literary Review* ("Colostomy Diaries," Fall 2011).

Thank you to the University of New Orleans Publishing Lab Prize for awarding GUTS as a finalist, and the judges of the following contests for essays excerpted in GUTS: *Parks and Points Essay Contest* (3rd place); *New Millennium Writers Contest* (Honorable mention); *Oregon Quarterly* Northwest Perspectives Essay Contest (Finalist); *The Atlantic* Student Writing Contest (Honorable mention); Artsmith Literary Award (Honorable mention).

# Vine Leaves Press

Enjoyed this book?
Go to *vineleavespress.com* to find more.